easy

Internet,
Third Edition

See it done

Do it yourself

QUe®

 Part ▶ **7:** Internet Phone Calls and Virtual Meetings

 Part ▶ **6:** Chatting on the Internet

 Part ▶ **8:** Creating and Publishing a Web Page

Copyright© 1998 by Que® Corporation

Screen reproductions in this book were created by means of the program Collage Complete from Inner Media, Inc., Hollis, NH.

Printed in the United States of America

International Standard Book Number: 0-7897-1639-9

Library of Congress Catalog Card Number: 98-84198

01   00   99   98   4

About the Author

Joe Kraynak has written dozens of successful computer books, including *The Complete Idiot's Guide to Netscape Communicator 4, Internet 6-in-1,* and *The Big Basics Book of the Internet.* Joe has a Master's degree from Purdue University.

Acknowledgments

Thanks to Jamie Milazzo, Lisa Wagner, Nadeem Muhammed, Gina Brown, Margaret Berson, Trina Wurst, Gary Adair, and to the illustrators for their hard work and expertise.

America Online screens reprinted with permission. Copyright 1997-98 America Online, Inc. All rights reserved.

mIRC home page and screens used with permission from Tjerk Vonck.

Internet Movie Database screens used with permission from Internet Movie Database Ltd. (www.IMDb.com).

Karl Jeacle's Mortgage Calculator used with permission from Karl Jeacle.

Virtual Mir, copyright Planet 9 Studios, San Francisco, CA (www.planet9.com).

BlackJack Java applet used with permission from Dmitry Vostokov.

CNET screens reprinted with permission from CNET, Inc. (Copyright 1995-98. www.cnet.com).

IQuest screens used with permission from IQuest Internet, Inc. (1-800-844-8649).

JavaScript Vehicle Auto Payment Calculator developed by Ryan Stone, Integon Corporation, 1997.

Olympic Movement Home Page reproduced with consent of the International Olympic Committee.

Microsoft, Amazon.com, PCTV.com, Dell, a-s, Costco, Yahoo!, Lycos, MSNBC, ESPN, Archie, CuteFTP, WorldsChat, White Pine, VeriSign, Business Week, Fortune

Executive Editor
Lisa Wagner

Acquisitions Editor
Jamie Milazzo

Technical Editor
Nadeem Muhammed

Managing Editor
Thomas F. Hayes

Project Editor
Gina Brown

Copy Editor
Margaret Berson

Indexer
Cheryl Jackson

Production Designer
Trina Wurst

Production
Lana Dominguez
Maribeth Echard

Book Designer
Jean Bisesi

Cover Designer
Anne Jones
Karen Ruggles

How to Use This Book

It's as Easy as 1-2-3

Each part of this book is made up of a series of short, instructional lessons, designed to help you understand basic information that you need to get the most out of your computer hardware and software.

 Click: Click the left mouse button once.

 Double-click: Click the left mouse button twice in rapid succession.

 Right-click: Click the right mouse button once.

 Pointer Arrow: Highlights an item on the screen you need to point to or focus on in the step or task.

 Selection: Highlights the area onscreen discussed in the step or task.

 Click & Type: Click once where indicated and begin typing to enter your text or data.

 Tips and Warnings give you a heads-up for any extra information you may need while working through the task.

2 Each task includes a series of quick, easy steps designed to guide you through the procedure.

 **Drag**

Drop

How to Drag: Point to the starting place or object. Hold down the mouse button (right or left per instructions), move the mouse to the new location, then release the button.

1 Each step is fully illustrated to show you how it looks onscreen.

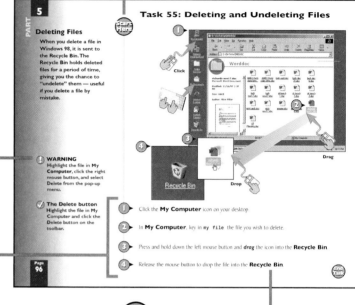

3 Items that you select or click in menus, dialog boxes, tabs, and windows are shown in **Bold**. Information you type is in a `special font`.

 Next Step: If you see this symbol, it means the task you're working on continues on the next page.

End Task: Task is complete.

Introduction to the Internet

The Internet is the largest network on the planet, connecting your computer to computers all over the world.

The interconnected nature of the Internet gives you access to resources stored on remote computers, including multimedia pages, audio and video clips, games, and programs. And, because the Internet connects you with other Internet users, you can exchange email, chat, join in discussion groups, and even make Internet phone calls to other people who are connected to the Internet.

- View multimedia Web pages.
- Send and receive mail.
- Chat with people from around the world.
- Call someone with Internet phone.

With an Internet connection, the right programs, and *Easy Internet, Third Edition*, as your roadmap, you have everything you need to get started. You'll be chatting up a storm and surfing like a pro in no time!

Connecting to the Internet

Before you can tap the power of the Internet, you must have a computer and an Internet connection. You can connect with a modem, over a network, or by using a special satellite dish or cable. The following tasks show you how to choose a connection type, find an Internet service provider, and set up your Internet connection.

Tasks

Pick a Connection Type

The most common way to connect to the Internet is to use a modem to dial a phone number that connects you to an online service (such as America Online or Prodigy) or to an Internet service provider (ISP). You can also use a network, satellite dish, or Internet cable service, for faster connections.

Modems
Satellite and cable connections carry signals only one way—to your computer or TV. You must still use a modem to transmit your input to the Internet.

Task 1: Locating an Internet Service Provider (ISP)

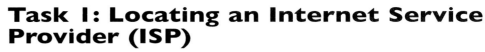

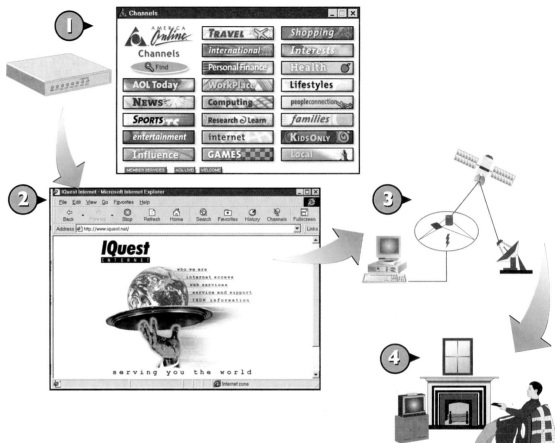

 Connect with a modem to a commercial online service.

 Connect to an Internet service provider's computer and use special software.

 Access the Web by satellite, with a satellite dish and modem connection.

 Use a WebTV box and remote to access the Internet on your TV.

Commercial Service Providers

America Online:
1-800-827-6364

CompuServe:
1-800-524-3388

The Microsoft Network:
1-800-FREE-MSN
1-800-373-3676

Prodigy:
1-800-PRODIGY
1-800-776-3449

Welcome to the **Microsoft Internet Referral Service**. From the list below, choose the service provider whose offer best fits your Internet needs.
If you need help figuring out what to do next, click here.

Microsoft

Premier Internet Service Providers

		More Info	Sign Me Up
Concentric Network Easy, reliable, ultra-fast, unlimited active Internet access in over 3,000 areas-$19.95/mo, Basic-$7.95/mo; No set-up fees. Great deals, Customizable Start/Home Pages, Email, news, games, chat, 24-hr customer support & more! Click here for 1st month FREE!			
IDT Corporation 2 FREE MONTHS: Featured in PC magazine, Wall Street Journal, NY Times etc. Rated #1 for network reliability by Smart Money magazine. $19.95 includes 1000's of newsgroups, 33.6 kbps 24/7 live tech support: Sign up and get 1st & 13th MONTHS FREE !!			
MCI Internet The easiest way to access the Internet! Quick and easy access to all the news, information and ideas you need 24 hours a day. Explore the Internet with unlimited access for only $19.95 a month. Sign up now and get the first month FREE!			
AT&T WorldNet Service World Class Award (PC World July 1997), First Place Ranking (Smart Money May 1997), MVP Award (PC Computing Nov. 1996), $19.95 a month unlimited usage, 1st. Month FREE! 24 Hour Support. Win weekly prizes and quarterly trips in our Travel the World Sweeps!			
Sprint Internet Passport Sprint Internet Passport Only ISP with the Get-Connected Guarantee-if we can't connect you, we'll credit you a week. Sprint's fiber optic network delivers fast, reliable connections. Rated #1 in page download speed (Inverse). First month FREE, then $19.95			
SPRYNET 1996 PC Magazine Editor's Choice Award for Best National ISP! $19.95/month unlimited pricing plan, 5MB free home page hosting, 24 hour online support, more local access points then any other ISP			

Find an ISP

After you determine how you want to connect to the Internet, you can begin to shop for a service. When shopping, compare subscription rates. Some services charge a flat rate for unlimited use. Others may charge rates based on time or amount of data delivered to your system. This can become quite costly.

Check the phone book for Internet service providers.

Call America Online, The Microsoft Network, CompuServe, or Prodigy.

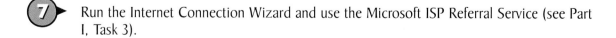
Run the Internet Connection Wizard and use the Microsoft ISP Referral Service (see Part I, Task 3).

Find a Satellite Service
For satellite service, call your local computer store and ask about *DirecPC*. DirecDuo offers a combination unit for TV and Web service.

Connect with America Online

Commercial services, such as America Online, popularized electronic communications. In addition to offering access to special features available only to members, these services now let you wander off to the Internet with a click of a button.

Task 2: Accessing the Internet from a Commercial Service

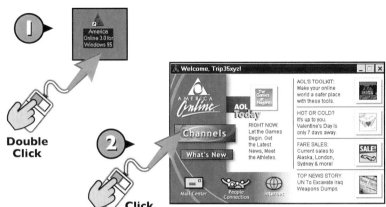

Double Click

Click

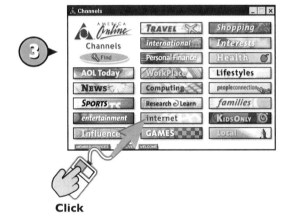

Click

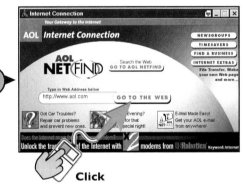

Click

✓ **Connect to the Web**
Press **Ctrl+K**, type web, and press **Enter** to quickly go to the World Wide Web on America Online.

1 ▶ Double-click the **America Online** shortcut icon, and sign on to America Online as you normally do.

2 ▶ In America Online, click **Channels**.

3 ▶ Click **Internet**.

4 ▶ Click the link for the Internet feature you want: **Go to the Web** or **Newsgroups**.

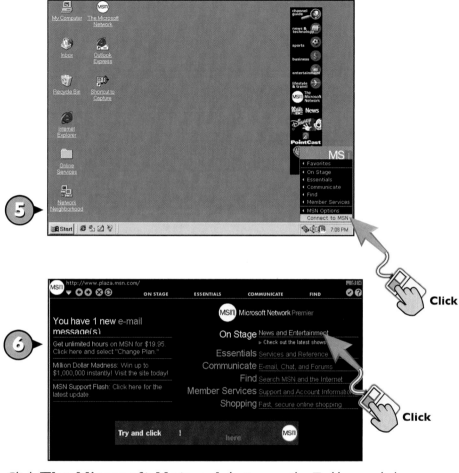

Click

Click

Connect with the Microsoft Network

When you sign on to the Microsoft Network, you are on the World Wide Web, a feature of the Internet that lets you jump from one page to another by clicking icons, buttons, or highlighted text, called *links*.

5 ▶ Click **The Microsoft Network** button on the Taskbar, and choose **Connect to MSN**.

6 ▶ Click buttons, icons, or links to open the desired page.

End Task

Find an ISP and Connect

The Internet Connection Wizard, included with Windows and other Microsoft products, automates your Internet setup. If you do not have an Internet service provider, the Wizard can help you find one, get the required software, and make the connection settings.

✓ **Run the Internet Connection Wizard**
You can run the Internet Connection Wizard by choosing **Start, Programs, Internet Explorer, Connection Wizard**.

✓ **Steps May Vary**
Microsoft's Internet Connection Wizard is being constantly updated, so the steps you must perform may differ.

Task 3: Using the Internet Connection Wizard

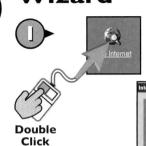

Start Here

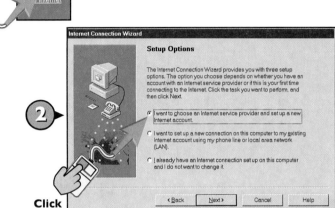

Double Click

Click

Click

Double-click **The Internet** or **Connect to the Internet**. (You may need to click **Next** to get the following options.)

Select **I Want to Choose an Internet Service Provider...**, and click **Next**. Select the default (topmost option), to choose an ISP or start a new account, and click **Next**.

Follow the onscreen instructions to pick an ISP and sign up for the desired service.

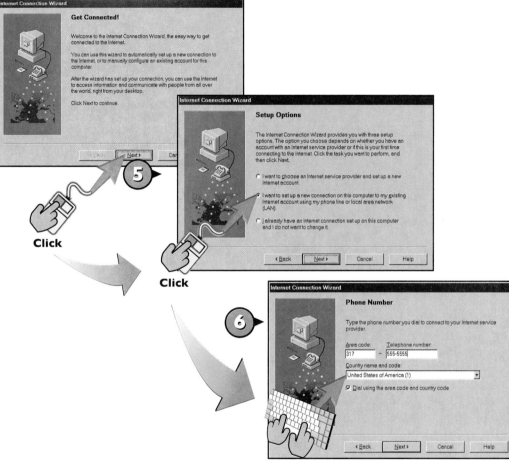

Connect to an Existing Account

If you already set up an account with an ISP, the Wizard can step you through the process of entering the required settings. Start the Wizard and follow the onscreen instructions.

Click

Click

Run the Internet Connection Wizard. (You may need to click **Next** to get the following options.)

Click the second option to set up a new connection for an account you already have.

Follow the onscreen instructions to enter the phone number and connection settings specified by your ISP.

✓ Enter Advanced Settings
When asked if you want to enter advanced settings, click **Yes** to check the settings against those specified by your service provider.

End Task

Create a New Connection Icon

If you don't have the Internet Connection Wizard, you must enter your ISP's connection settings manually in Windows Dial-Up Networking or the program you use to connect to the Internet. Dial-Up Networking is used here as an example.

Task 4: Entering Internet Connection Settings Manually

Start Here

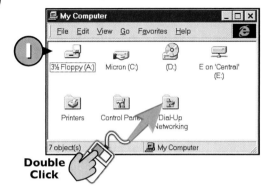

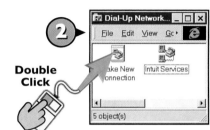

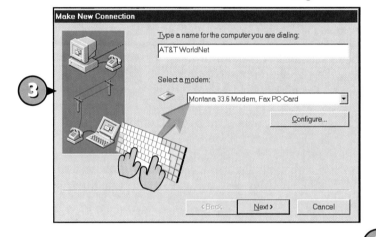

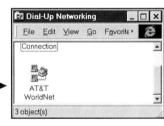

Open **My Computer** and double-click **Dial-Up Networking**.

Double-click **Make New Connection**.

Follow the onscreen instructions to select your modem and enter the phone number of your service provider's computer.

When you are done, you have a new icon for your service provider.

Next Step

Enter Connection Settings

Before you can use your new icon to connect to your ISP, you must enter the connection settings that your ISP specified. You must have the following information from your ISP: phone number, logon name and password, server type (PPP or SLIP), domain name, Domain Name Server (DNS) address (if required), and IP address (if required).

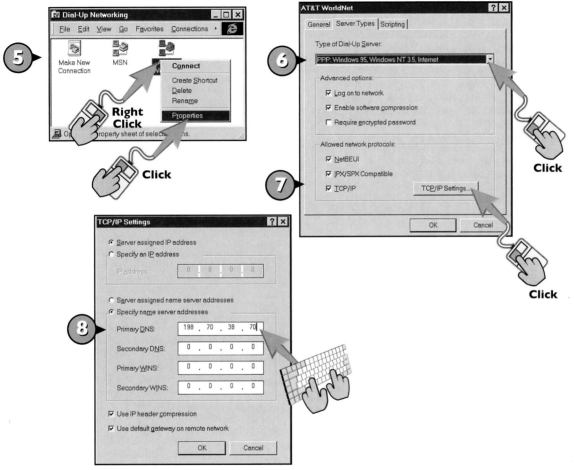

 Right-click the **Dial-Up Networking** icon you created, and choose **Properties**.

 Click the **Server Types** tab, and make sure the correct Dial-Up Server type is selected: PPP or SLIP.

 Click the **TCP/IP Settings** button.

 If your ISP requires you to use a specific IP address or DNS address, enter those addresses.

Wrong DNS Address
If you enter the wrong DNS address, when you attempt to open any Web page, your Web browser will indicate that it cannot find the specified page.

Task 5: Logging On and Off the Internet

Connect to the Internet

Before you can use an Internet program for navigating the Web, sending or reading email, joining discussion groups, or performing any other task, you must establish an Internet connection. You do this by dialing the number specified by your ISP and entering your username and password. Here, you learn how to connect with **Dial-Up Networking**.

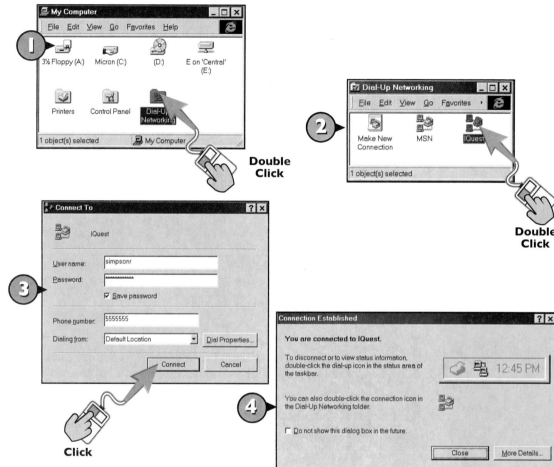

✓ **Internet Connections**
Many Internet programs automatically connect you to the Internet when you start them. Others may prompt you to connect. Some programs may not work unless you first establish a connection.

1 ▶ Open **My Computer** and double-click **Dial-Up Networking**.

2 ▶ Double-click the Dial-Up Networking icon you created.

3 ▶ Enter your username and password, and click **Connect**.

4 ▶ Dial-Up Networking dials in to your service provider's computer and connects you.

Next Step

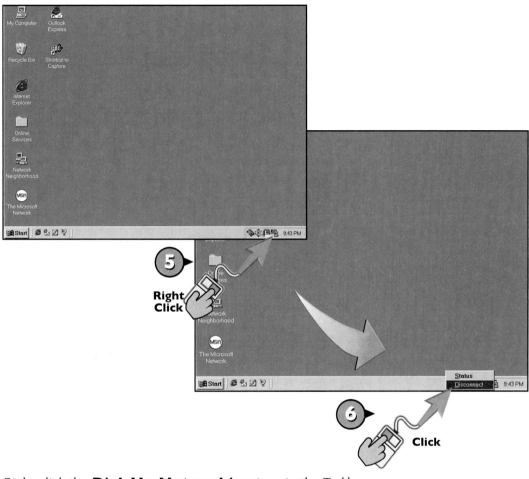

Disconnect from the Internet

After your computer is connected to the Internet, you can close the Connected To dialog box to get it out of the way. (Closing the dialog box does not hang up.) You can then run your Internet programs. When you are done using the Internet, you should disconnect.

5 ▶ Right-click the **Dial-Up Networking** icon in the Taskbar.

6 ▶ Choose **Disconnect**.

Browsing the World Wide Web

The World Wide Web (Web for short) is a huge multimedia document with pages stored on computers all over the world. These pages contain text, graphics, animated clips, audio and video clips, games, order forms, and just about anything else you can imagine. Using a special program called a Web browser, you can open and navigate these Web pages. The following tasks show you just what to do.

Tasks

Downloading and Installing Internet Explorer

Before you start opening Web pages, you should make sure you have the latest version of your Web browser. You can use your current Web browser to download Microsoft's Internet Explorer, a suite of programs that features a Web browser, email, newsgroups, chat, Internet phone, and Web page editing.

✓ **Update Internet Explorer**
To ensure that you have all the updated Internet Explorer 4 components, open Internet Explorer's **Help** menu and choose **Product Updates**.

✓ **Run Internet Explorer**
After installing Internet Explorer, you can run it by clicking its icon on the desktop or by choosing it from **Start, Programs, Internet Explorer**.

Task 1: Downloading and Installing an Up-to-Date Web Browser

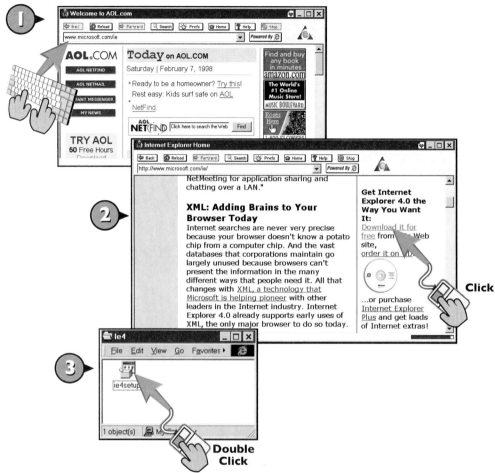

Click in the Web page address text box in your Web browser, type **www.microsoft.com/ie**, and press **Enter**.

Click the **Download** link, and follow the onscreen instructions to download the file.

When the download is complete, double-click the file's icon and follow the onscreen installation instructions. (You must be connected to the Internet.)

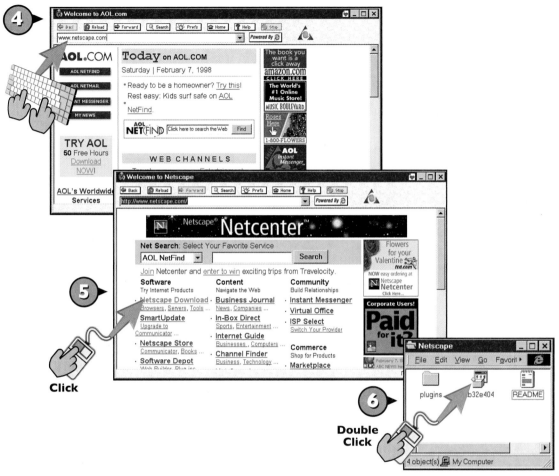

Click

Double
Click

Downloading and Installing Netscape Communicator

Netscape Communicator also features a suite of programs that includes a Web browser, email, newsgroups, instant messages, Internet phone, and Web page editing. You can download Communicator from Netscape's Web site.

✓ Run Netscape Communicator
After installing Netscape Communicator, you can run it by double-clicking its icon on the desktop or by choosing **Start, Programs, Netscape Communicator**.

! Get Communicator
Make sure you download Netscape Communicator, which includes email, newsgroups, and other useful components, in addition to **Navigator** (the Web browser).

④▶ Click in the Web page address text box in your Web browser, type **www.netscape.com**, and press **Enter**.

⑤▶ Click the **Netscape Download** link, and follow the onscreen instructions to download Netscape Communicator.

⑥▶ When the download is complete, double-click the file's icon to install Netscape Communicator.

End Task

Task 2: Browsing Web Pages with Links

Clicking Links

Most Web pages have icons, buttons, and highlighted text, called **links** (or **hyperlinks**). You click a link to open another Web page, play media files, or copy files to your computer. You can then use the **Back** and **Forward** buttons to return to the pages you most recently visited.

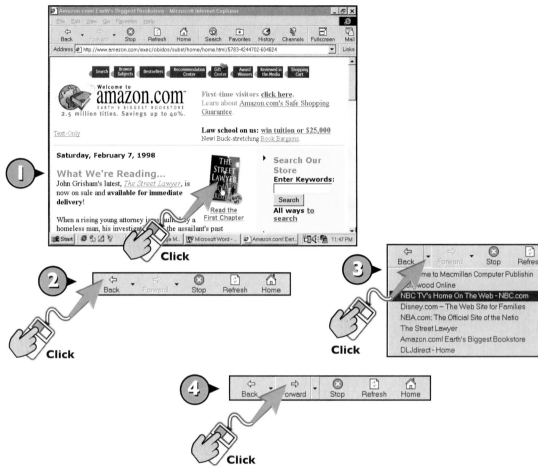

Click

Click

Click

Click

✓ **Image Maps**
Some Web pages use large graphics, called image maps, for navigation. Each area of the image points to a different page.

✓ **Quick Back and Forward**
Press **Alt+←** to move back or **Alt+→** to move forward.

① Move the mouse pointer over a button, icon, or highlighted text, and click.

② To move back to a page you opened, click the **Back** button.

③ Click the down arrow to the right of the **Back** button, and choose the desired page (click and hold the button in Netscape Navigator).

④ If you back up, you can click the **Forward** button to move ahead.

Task 3: Opening a Web Page Using an Address (URL)

Click

Entering a Web Page Address

Each Web page has its own *address*, also called an *URL (Uniform Resource Locator)*. You can open a specific page if you know its address by entering the address in the Address, Location, or Go To text box above the page viewing area.

1 Click in the **Address**, **Location**, or **Go To** text box.

2 Type the address of the page you want to open, and press **Enter**.

✅ **AutoComplete**
With AutoComplete, type a few characters of the address of a page you have already visited, and AutoComplete inserts the rest—just press **Enter**.

✅ **Type Less**
You can omit the http:// at the beginning of an address. Your Web browser inserts it for you.

Task 4: Returning to Pages You Visited

Using the Address List

The Address, Go To, or Location text box doubles as a drop-down list that displays the addresses of pages you have recently opened. You can quickly return to a page by selecting it from this list.

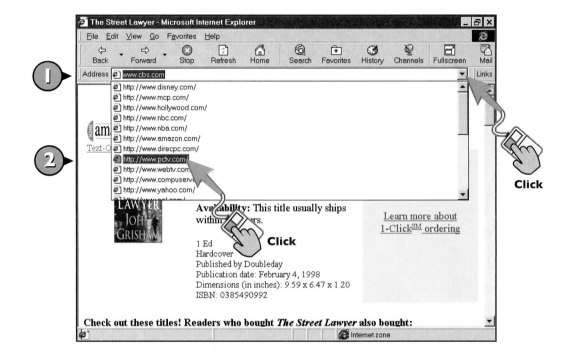

Click

Click

Big Screen View
In Internet Explorer, click the **Fullscreen** button to give the Web page the entire viewing area.

 Click the arrow to the right of the Address, Go To, or Location text box.

 Click the address of the desired page.

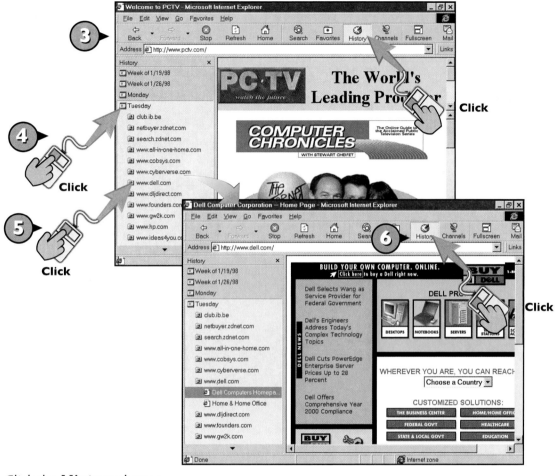

Using a History List

The history list provides a more comprehensive record of your Web journeys. In Internet Explorer, click the **History** button to display a log of your Web wanderings. Click the day or week when you opened the page, and click the page's name.

③ ► Click the **History** button.

④ ► Click the week or day on which you opened the page.

⑤ ► Click the page's name.

⑥ ► Click the **History** button again to close the pane.

✔ **Navigator History List**
In Netscape Navigator, open the **Communicator** menu and choose **History,** or press **Ctrl+H** to view the history list.

Task 5: Navigating Frames

Working on a Framed Page

Some Web pages you encounter may use *frames*, which divide the browser window into two or more panes to help you navigate. Typically, the pane on the left contains an outline of the site with links. You can then click a link to view another page without having to back up.

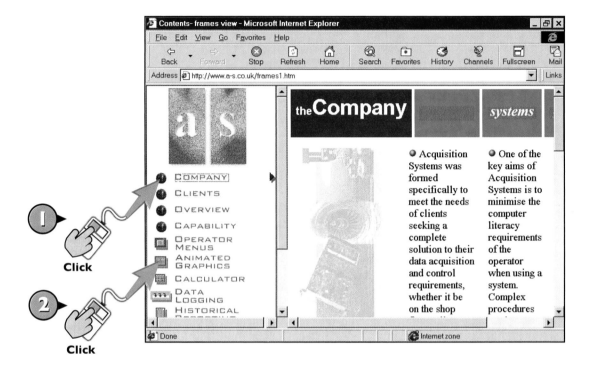

Click

Click

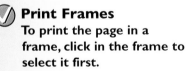

Print Frames
To print the page in a frame, click in the frame to select it first.

1 ► Click the link in the left frame to view the linked page in the right frame.

2 ► Click another link to display a different page in the right frame.

Task 6: Completing Online Forms

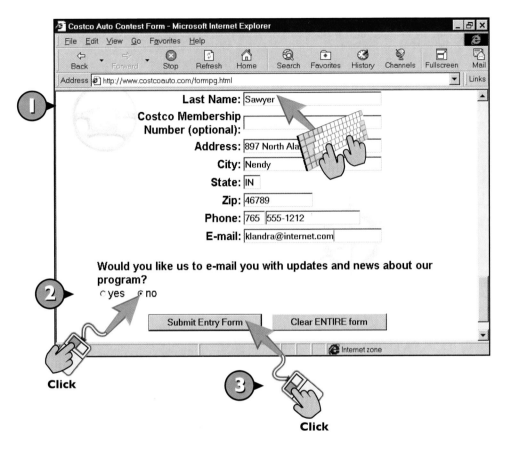

Click

Click

Typing Entries in Forms

Many Web pages use forms to allow you to provide feedback, search for terms, order products, and register for contests. To complete a form, just pretend that the form is a big dialog box, complete with text boxes, lists, and command buttons.

1. Click in the text box, and type your entry.

2. Select options or list items.

3. Click a command button to submit your entry.

Tab to It
In some forms, you can press the Tab key to move from one blank to another.

Task 7: Finding Information with Web Search Tools

Searching Yahoo!

Yahoo! is one of the most popular search tools for finding pages on the Web. You enter a word or two to describe what you are looking for, and Yahoo! delivers a list of links to categories and specific sites that match your entry.

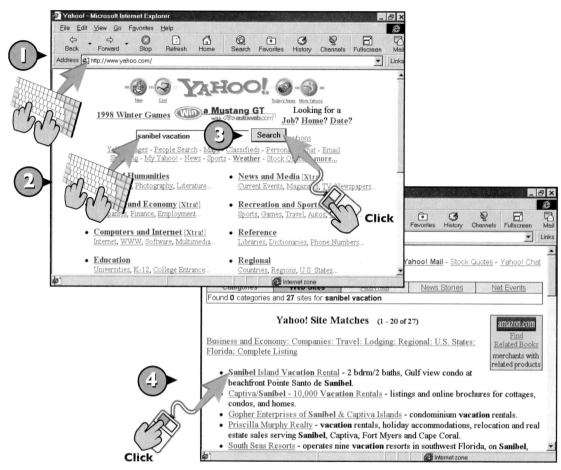

 More Search Tools
Click your Web browser's **Search** button to display additional search tools.

 Jump to Other Search Pages
After you perform a search using Yahoo!, you may find links to other popular search tools following the Yahoo! search results.

 Type **www.yahoo.com** in the Address or Location text box, and press **Enter**.

 Click in the text box at the top of the page, and type your search phrase.

Click the **Search** button.

Click the link for the page you want to open.

 Next Step

Searching Lycos

Lycos is another popular Internet search tool. Lycos allows you to narrow your search by selecting a specific area of the Internet: the Web, discussion groups, weather, and so on.

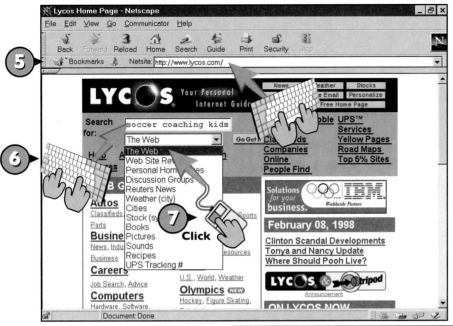

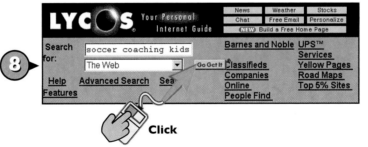

5 ▶ Type **www.lycos.com** in the Address or Location text box, and press **Enter**.

6 ▶ Click in the text box at the top of the page, and type your search phrase.

7 ▶ Choose the area of the Internet you want to search.

8 ▶ Click **Go Get It**.

✓ Narrow Your Search
Enclose your search phrase in quotes to have Lycos look for the phrase exactly as you typed it. Use a plus sign (+) between words to narrow the search.

End Task

Task 8: Finding People on the Web

Searching Four11

The Web has several online phone books that you can use to look up email addresses, home addresses, and phone numbers of your long-lost friends and relatives. You can even get directions to people's homes. Four11 is one of the more popular people-search tools.

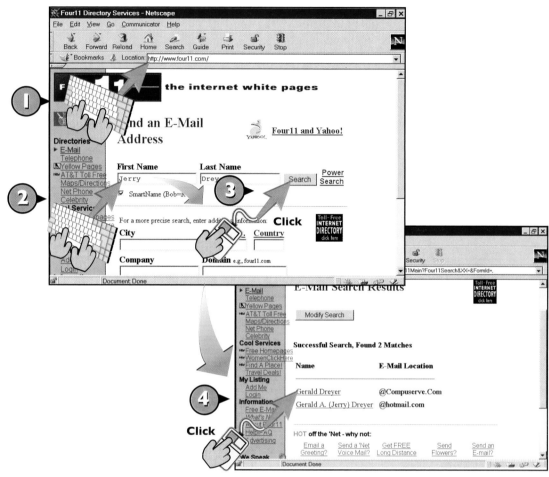

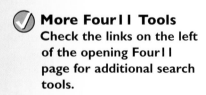

More Four11 Tools
Check the links on the left of the opening Four11 page for additional search tools.

 Type **www.four11.com** in the text box above the Web page, and press **Enter**.

 Type the person's first and last name and any other information that will help locate the person.

 Click the **Search** button.

 Click the person's link for more information.

Searching WhoWhere

WhoWhere is another popular search tool for tracking down people. In addition to helping you find people, WhoWhere can help you find an apartment, job, car, and other items you might need.

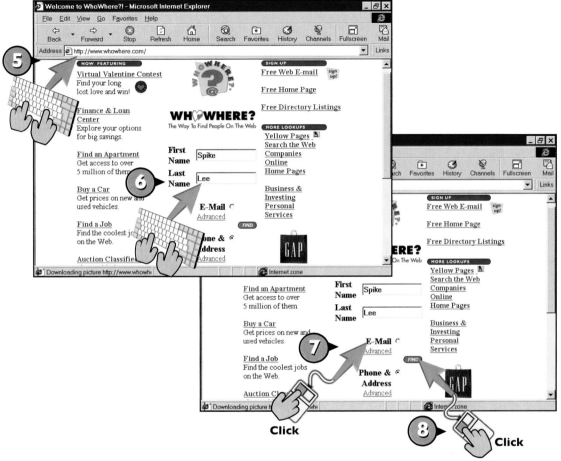

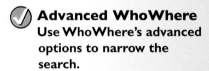

Click

Click

5 ▶ Type **www.whowhere.com** in the text box above the Web page, and press **Enter**.

6 ▶ Type the person's first and last name in the text boxes.

7 ▶ Click **Email** or **Phone & Address**.

8 ▶ Click **Find**.

✓ **Advanced WhoWhere**
Use WhoWhere's advanced options to narrow the search.

Task 9: Marking Your Favorite Pages for Quick Return Trips

Adding Pages to Favorites Menu

As you skip from page to page on the Web, you may find pages you want to return to later. Locating the page again may be difficult, because you may not remember the address or the trail of links you had to follow. The solution is to add the page to your Favorites menu in Internet Explorer.

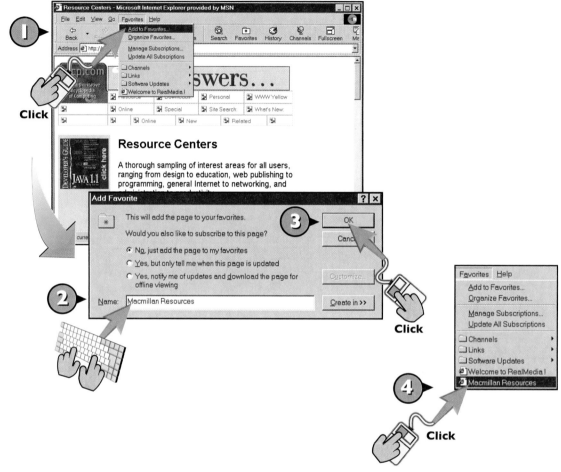

✓ Favorites Pane
Click the **Favorites** button to display the contents of the Favorites menu in the left pane.

✓ Start, Favorites
Your marked pages also appear on the **Start, Favorites** menu.

 Open the desired page, and then open the **Favorites** menu and choose **Add to Favorites**.

 To change the name as it appears on the Favorites menu, drag over the **Name** entry and type a new name.

 Click **OK**.

 You can return to the page at any time by selecting it from the **Favorites** menu.

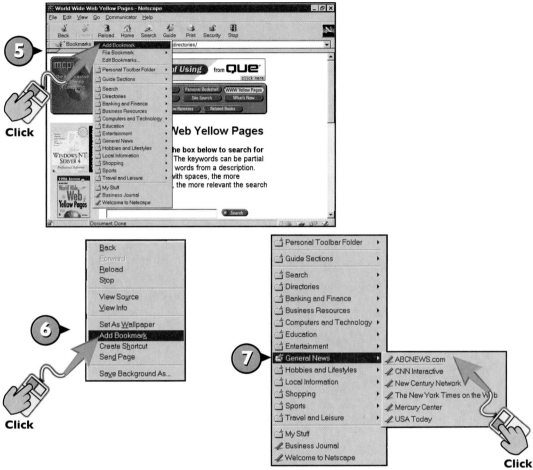

Click

Click

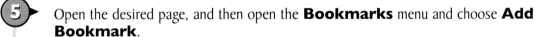

Click

Click

Flagging Pages with Bookmarks

Netscape Navigator allows you to add page names to the Bookmarks menu, so you can quickly return to them later. Navigator offers several ways to add bookmarks, as shown in these steps.

✅ **Quick Bookmarks**
To quickly add the currently open page to the bottom of the Bookmarks menu, press **Ctrl+D**.

✅ **Desktop Shortcut**
To add a shortcut icon for the page to the Windows desktop, right-click the page or a link and choose **Create Shortcut**.

5 ▶ Open the desired page, and then open the **Bookmarks** menu and choose **Add Bookmark**.

6 ▶ Right-click a link or a blank area of the page, and choose **Add Bookmark**.

7 ▶ Drag a link over **Bookmarks**, over a subfolder name, and onto the subfolder and release the mouse button.

End Task

Task 10: Organizing Bookmarks and Favorites

Start Here

Reorganizing Favorites

As you add pages to the Favorites menu, the menu may become cluttered. To clean up the menu, you can remove pages or create your own submenus and move related pages to the submenus.

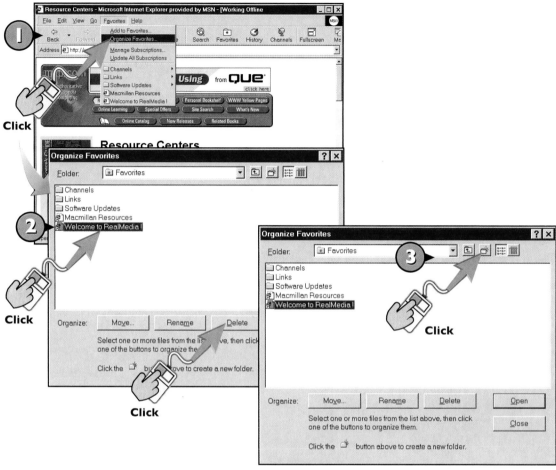

Click

Click

Click

Click

✓ **Reorganize Shortcuts**
You can drag favorites from the Favorites folder to subfolders to move them.

✓ **Manage Shortcuts**
The Organize Favorites window is like the My Computer window. Use the same techniques for selecting, moving, and deleting Favorites that you use for managing files.

1 ▶ Open the **Favorites** menu and choose **Organize Favorites**.

2 ▶ Click a page to remove it from the menu, and click the **Delete** button.

3 ▶ Click the **Create New Folder** button to create a folder that will act as a submenu, and then type a name for the folder.

Next Step

Reorganizing Bookmarks

When you add a bookmark, Navigator inserts it at the bottom of the Bookmarks menu, which can make the menu too long. You can delete bookmarks or add them to submenus to make the Bookmarks menu more manageable.

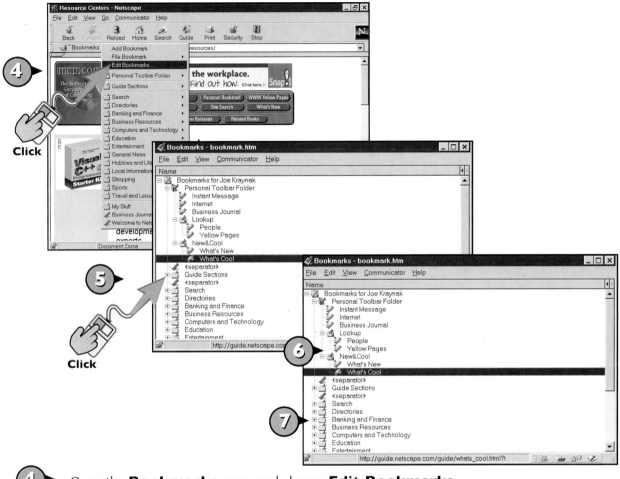

(4) Open the **Bookmarks** menu and choose **Edit Bookmarks**.

(5) Click the plus sign next to a folder to display its contents.

(6) You can drag bookmarks up or down to move them or select a bookmark and press **Delete** to remove it.

(7) To place a bookmark in a subfolder, drag the bookmark over the subfolder's icon.

✓ **Quick Access to the Bookmarks Window**
Press **Ctrl+B** to display the Bookmarks window.

✓ **Bookmarks Submenu**
In the Bookmarks window, open the **File** menu and choose **New Folder** to create a new Bookmarks submenu.

Task 11: Subscribing to Web Sites

In Internet Explorer, you can subscribe to Web pages as you add them to your Favorites menu. At the scheduled time, Internet Explorer automatically connects to the Web site, retrieves the specified page(s), and disconnects. You can then view the pages offline (without connecting to the Internet).

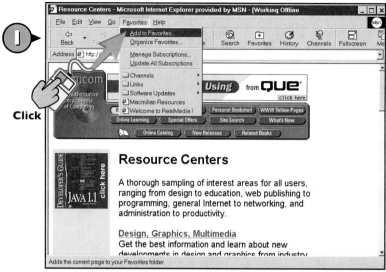

Click

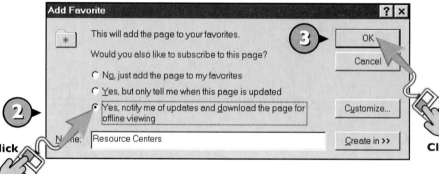

Click

Click

✓ **Customize Favorite**
Click the **Customize** button in the Add Favorite dialog box to specify when you want Internet Explorer to get the page.

✓ **Cancel Subscriptions**
To cancel subscriptions, open the **Favorites** menu and choose **Manage Subscriptions**.

 Open the **Favorites** menu and choose **Add to Favorites**.

 Click **Yes, Notify Me of Updates...**.

Click **OK**.

Task 12: Browsing the Web Offline

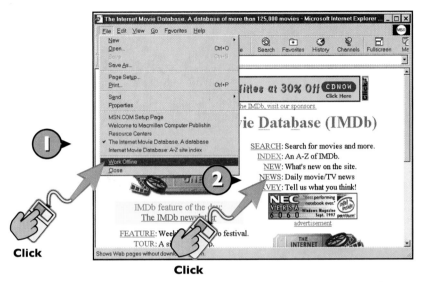

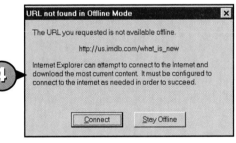

Viewing Pages Offline

Whenever you open a page, your Web browser stores it in a temporary storage area on your hard disk, called the *cache* (pronounced "cash"). If you subscribe to Web sites, the downloaded pages are also placed on your hard disk. You can then open the pages from your hard disk without connecting to the Internet.

Click

Click

 Open your Web browser's **File** menu, choose **Go Offline** or **Work Offline**, and then disconnect from the Internet.

 Open pages as you normally would, entering page addresses and clicking links.

 If you move the mouse pointer over a link for a page that is not on your hard disk, a "not" sign appears next to the pointer.

 If you click the link anyway, your Web browser indicates that you are working offline and prompts you to connect.

✅ **Start Offline**
To start your Web browser in Offline mode, run your browser and then click **Cancel** in the Connect To dialog box.

Task 13: Playing Java Applets

Playing a Java Applet

Java is a programming language commonly used on the Web to enhance Web pages and make them more interactive. Java is popular, because a Java applet can run on many different systems: for example, on a Macintosh running MacOS or a PC running Windows. You might encounter Java applets that let you play games, such as tic-tac-toe, or calculate refinance options for your home.

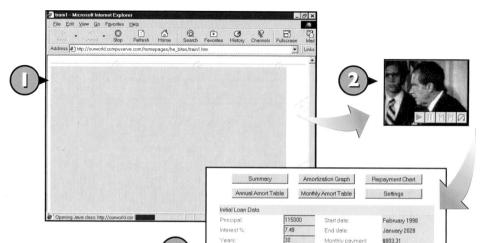

✓ **More Java Applets**
Look for links to Java applets at www.jars.com.

✓ **Java Chat**
Yahoo! uses Java to allow people to chat on the Web.

1 ▶ When you open a page that contains a Java applet, the page may display a gray box while your browser downloads the applet.

2 ▶ The applet may play a sound, video clip, or animation.

3 ▶ Some Java applets request your input.

4 ▶ Other applets may let you play a game or chat.

Next Step

Exploring JavaScript

Like Java, JavaScript enables Web page authors to enhance their Web pages. Web developers can type JavaScript commands right inside their Web pages, making it possible for people with little programming knowledge to enhance their Web pages.

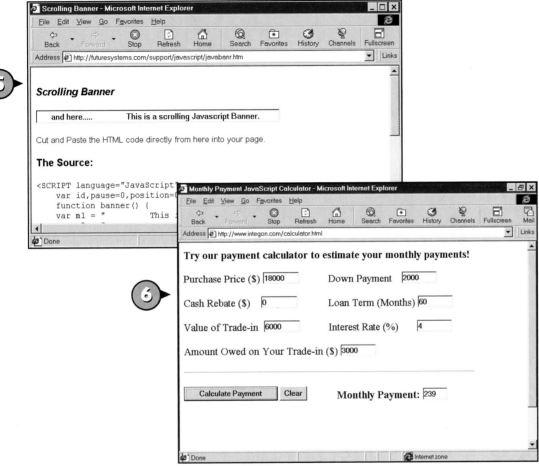

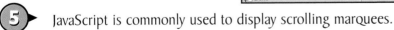

JavaScript is commonly used to display scrolling marquees.

You can find examples of more sophisticated JavaScript applications.

Disable Java
Java applets and JavaScript have built-in controls that prevent programmers from inserting viruses, but they still pose a slight risk. If you are concerned, you can disable Java in your Web browser (see Part 2, Tasks 17 and 18).

More JavaScript
Find more Java and JavaScript examples at www.gamelan.com.

Using Internet Explorer ActiveX Controls

ActiveX controls are add-on programs for your Web browser that enable the browser to play special content on Web pages. For example, the Shockwave ActiveX control can play interactive, multimedia Shockwave presentations. When you open a Web page that has ActiveX content, Internet Explorer prompts you to download and install the required control.

Safe ActiveX
To prevent viruses, do not download an ActiveX control unless a certificate pops up, assuring you that the control is safe. Most controls from recognized companies are safe.

ActiveX in Navigator
You can add ActiveX support to Netscape Navigator by installing a special plug-in from www.ncompasslabs.com.

Task 14: Downloading and Install ActiveX Controls

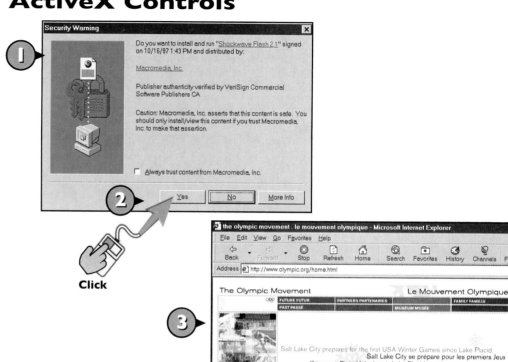

Click

When you connect to a Web page that has ActiveX content, Internet Explorer can download the required control.

Make sure the control has been certified before giving your okay, and then click **Yes**. If the ActiveX control has not been certified, cancel the download.

The ActiveX component plays right on the Web page.

Task 15: Downloading and Installing Plug-Ins

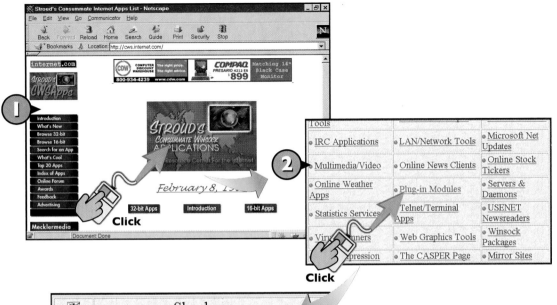

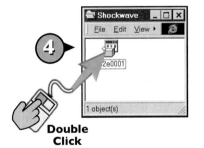

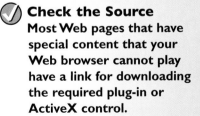

Click

Click

Click

Double Click

Getting Netscape Navigator Plug-Ins

Netscape Navigator cannot play all the media file types it encounters on the Web. To play files that Netscape Navigator cannot play, you must download and install a plug-in. You can find links to popular plug-ins at `browserwatch.internet.com/plug-in.html` `cws.internet.com` `www.tucows.com`

✓ **Installed Plug-Ins**
Find out which plug-ins are installed. Open the **Help** menu and choose **About Plug-ins**.

✓ **Check the Source**
Most Web pages that have special content that your Web browser cannot play have a link for downloading the required plug-in or ActiveX control.

Connect to `cws.internet.com`, and click the **Stroud's** graphic at the top center of the page.

Scroll down the page and click **Plug-in Modules**.

Scroll down the page, click the link next to **Location**, and save the file to a folder on your disk.

4 ▶ After the plug-in file is downloaded to the selected folder, double-click its icon to install it.

Task 16: Exploring 3D Worlds with VRML

Downloading and Installing a VRML Browser

VRML (pronounced "vermal") is short for **Virtual Reality Modeling Language, a programming language that enables developers to create three-dimensional worlds on the Web. To view VRML worlds, you need a VRML browser. Here's a list of VRML browsers you can try:**
Microsoft VRML (ActiveX):
`www.microsoft.com/ie/ie40/`
`download/addon.htm`
Cosmo Player (Netscape):
`cosmo.sgi.com`
Community Place:
`http://vs.spiw.com/vs/`
Platinum WIRL:
`www.platinum.com/products/`
`appdev/vream/wirl_ps.htm`

✓ **VRML Player Installed?**
If you are using Internet Explorer, Microsoft's **VRML viewer may already be installed. Try to open a VRML world and see what happens!**

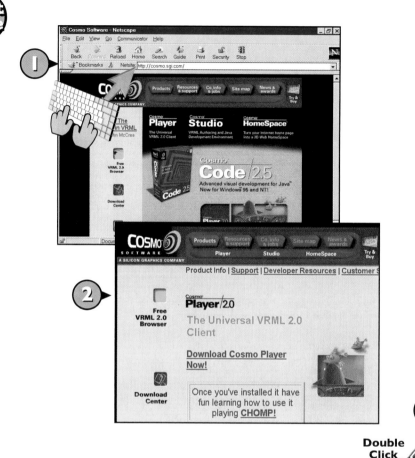

Enter the address of the Web site for the VRML browser you want to download.

Follow the instructions at the Web site to download the VRML browser to a folder on your hard disk.

Double-click the file you downloaded to install the VRML browser. (You may need to exit your Web browser first.)

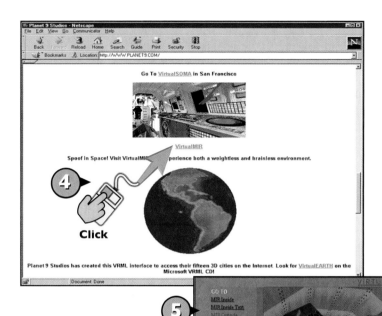

Opening a VRML World

When you have a VRML browser, you can use it to start exploring virtual worlds on the Web. Using your favorite search tool, search for VRML worlds. When you find a link to a VRML world, click it. Your Web browser automatically launches the VRML browser and displays the VRML page. Or check out the following VRML worlds:
Planet 9 Studios:
www.planet9.com
Yahoo! 3D:
3d.yahoo.com/3d/yahoo3d.html
Square USA:
www.sqla.com/~shiro/VRML/
Cybertown:
www.cybertown.com

Click

4 ▶ Click the link for the virtual world you want to visit.

5 ▶ The VRML world appears in your browser window.

6 ▶ In most VRML browsers, you drag inside the world to move around.

7 ▶ Use the VRML browser's controls to navigate.

Big Worlds
VRML worlds consist of large files. Even over a fast modem connection, navigation is slow.

Task 17: Customizing Internet Explorer

Entering General Settings

Internet Explorer offers several options for controlling it and changing the way it displays Web pages. You can choose to have Internet Explorer start with your favorite Web page, use less disk space for temporary files, or use different colors for Web page backgrounds and text.

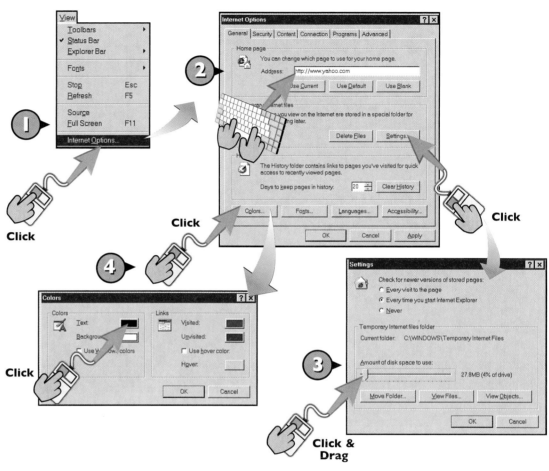

Click

Click

Click

Click

Click & Drag

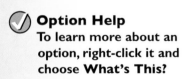

Option Help
To learn more about an option, right-click it and choose **What's This?**

 Open the **View** menu and choose **Internet Options**.

 In the **Address** text box, type the address of the Web page you want Internet Explorer to always open first. Click the **Settings** button.

 Drag the slider to specify how much disk space Internet Explorer should use.

 Click the **Colors** button, and choose the desired background, text, and links colors.

Next Step

Entering Advanced Settings

Although you may not want to change many options on the Internet Option dialog box's Advanced tab, you should check them out. You'll find options for excluding media files (for quicker page downloads), disabling Java (for increased security), starting Internet Explorer in Fullscreen mode, and much more.

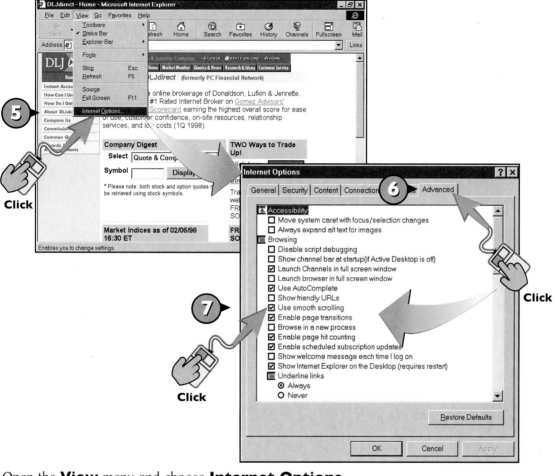

Click

Click

Click

Open the **View** menu and choose **Internet Options**.

Click the **Advanced** tab.

Click check box and option buttons to set your preferences, and click **OK**.

✓ **Security and Censors**
To secure your system, see Part 2, Task 19. To filter Web content, see Part 2, Task 20.

Configuring Navigator

Netscape Navigator's Preferences dialog box includes options for controlling the appearance and behavior of all the programs that make up the Communicator suite, including email and newsgroups. Here, you learn how to change common browser preferences.

Task 18: Customizing Netscape Navigator

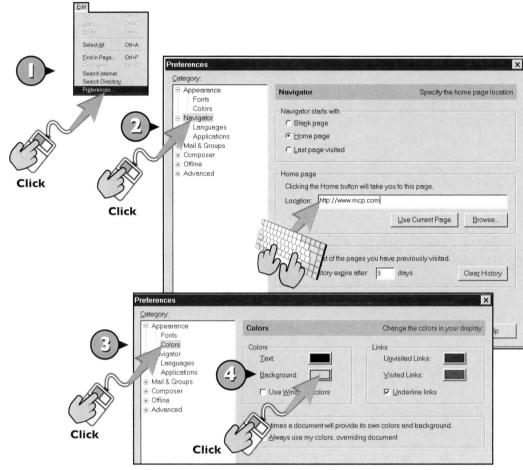

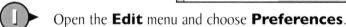

✓ Start Where You Left Off

To have Navigator open the last page that was opened when you exited Navigator, choose **Last Page Visited**.

1. Open the **Edit** menu and choose **Preferences**.

2. Click **Navigator**, and specify the Web page you want it to open on startup.

3. Click the plus sign next to **Appearance**, and click **Colors**.

4. Enter the desired colors for the page background, text, and links.

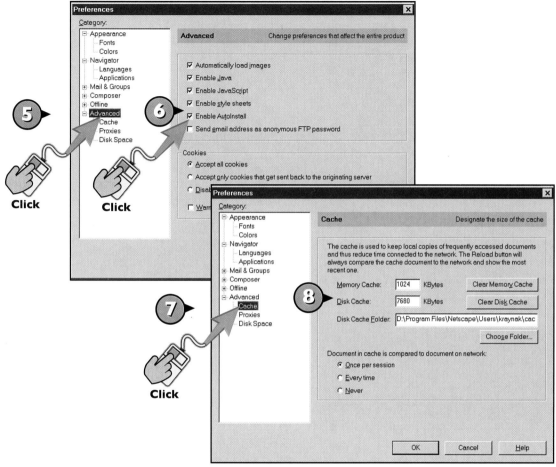

Entering Advanced Preferences

Navigator has several advanced options, which allow you to exclude graphics (for quick page loading); disable Java, JavaScript, and AutoInstall of plug-ins (for increased security); and change the cache size to free up memory and disk space. Click the **Help** button for details about the available options.

✓ **Speedy Return Trips**
To improve the speed at which Navigator loads pages you have previously visited, increase the cache sizes.

✓ **Faster, Text-Only Pages**
Turn off **Automatically Load Images** for speedier navigation. When you reach the desired page, click the **Images** button in Navigator's toolbar.

5 ▶ In the Preference dialog box, click **Advanced**.

6 ▶ Click the check boxes and option buttons to change any of the advanced settings.

7 ▶ Click the plus sign next to Advanced, and click **Cache**.

8 ▶ Enter settings to specify the amount of memory and disk space Navigator should use for temporary storage.

Task 19: Entering Security Settings

Configuring Internet Explorer Security

Internet Explorer uses four security zones to protect you on the Web: **Local Intranet** for network administrators, **Trusted Sites** to relax security for sites you trust, **Restricted Sites** to tighten security for sites you don't trust, and **Internet** for all other sites. You can change the security levels for each zone.

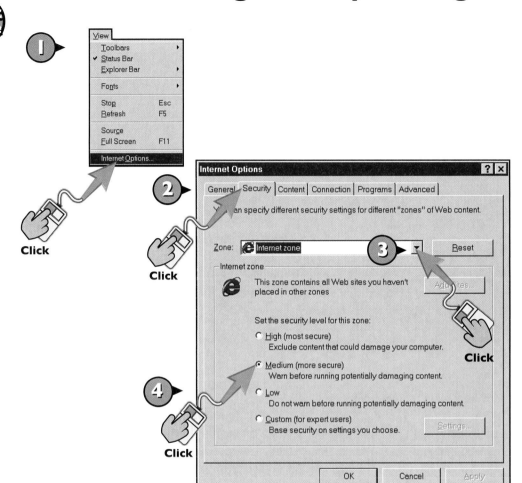

✓ **Too Many Warnings?**
To prevent warnings from popping up on sites you trust, choose the **Trusted Sites** zone, click the **Add Sites** button, and type the addresses of the sites you trust.

✓ **Look for the Lock**
When you open a secure Web form, a padlock icon appears in the status bar at the bottom of the window.

1 ▶ Open the **View** menu and choose **Internet Options**.

2 ▶ Click the **Security** tab.

3 ▶ Choose the desired security zone.

4 ▶ Choose the desired security level for the selected zone to tighten or relax security.

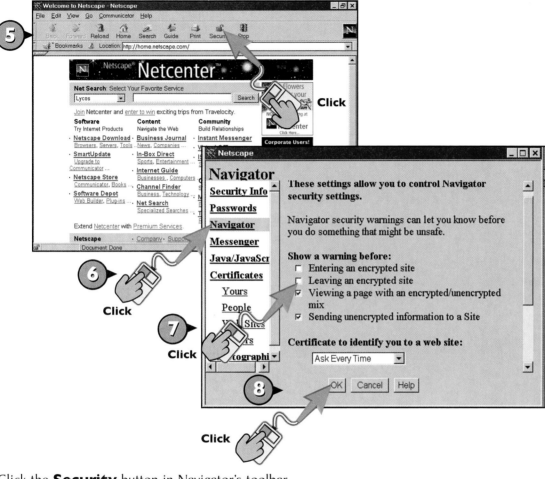

Configuring Navigator Security

Navigator's security features notify you if you are about to submit information using an insecure form. After some time, the warnings can become intrusive. If you are careful, consider disabling some of the security warnings, such as the warning that appears when you open a secure form.

5 Click the **Security** button in Navigator's toolbar.

6 Click **Navigator** in the list of security options.

7 Click the desired check boxes to disable any of the security warnings.

8 Click **OK**.

✓ **Find the Broken Key**
If you turn off the security warnings, you can still determine if a form is insecure. Navigator's status bar displays a broken key icon at insecure sites and an unbroken icon at secure sites.

Task 20: Censoring the Internet

Filtering Content in Internet Explorer

If you are in charge of children, you may want to restrict access to offensive sites. Internet Explorer has a built-in censor, called the **Content Advisor**, that can prevent Web pages that offer undesirable content, but you first have to turn it on.

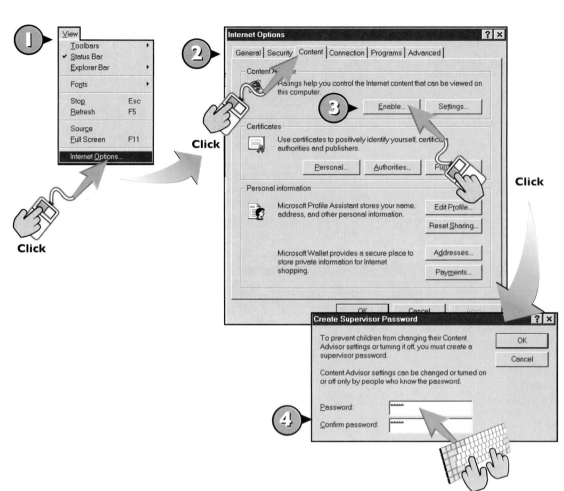

Click

Click

Click

Click

 Access Unrated Sites
Content Advisor blocks access to any unrated sites, which may contain valuable, inoffensive content. To permit access to unrated sites, click the **Settings** button and enter your preferences.

 Open the **View** menu and choose **Internet Options**.

 Click the **Content** tab.

 Click the **Enable** button.

4 Type your password in the **Password** and **Confirm Password** text boxes, and click **OK**.

Getting a Special Censoring Program

If you use a Web browser that does not have a built-in censor, you can download a censoring program from the Web. Following is a list of shareware (try-before-you-buy) programs you should check out:

Cyber Patrol:
www.cyberpatrol.com
CYBERsitter:
www.solidoak.com
Net Nanny:
www.netnanny.com

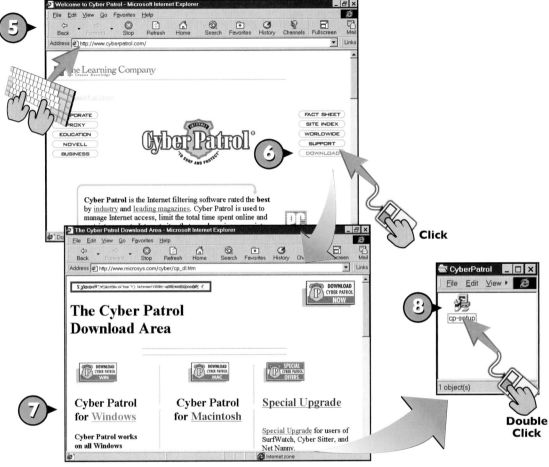

Click

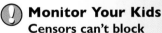

Double Click

---

5 ▶ Open CyberPatrol's home page at **www.cyberpatrol.com**.

6 ▶ Click the **Download** link.

7 ▶ Follow the Web site's instructions to download the shareware version of CyberPatrol.

8 ▶ After downloading the file, double-click its icon to install CyberPatrol.

Monitor Your Kids
Censors can't block everything, and sometimes they block access to valuable educational sites. You should still supervise your students or children.

End Task

Task 21: Tuning In to the Web with Netscape Netcaster

Running Netcaster

Netscape Netcaster allows Web developers to broadcast (push) Web content to your computer. You can then skip from one Web page to another as easily as flipping channels with your TV's remote control.

Start Here

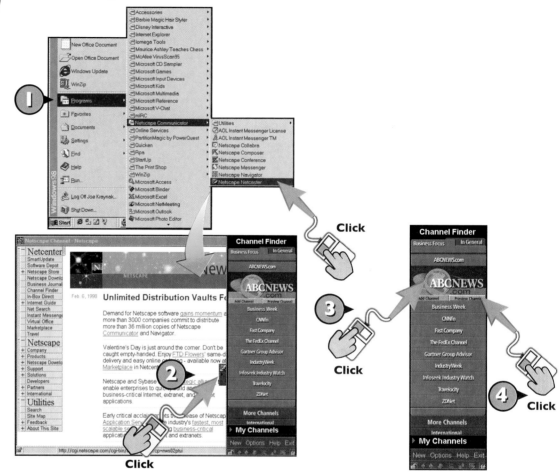

✓ **Free Delivery with Push Content**
Push content is a relatively new technology that allows Web developers to send Web pages to you without your having to request the pages.

✓ **Netcaster Quick Access**
To run Netcaster from Navigator, open the **Communicator** menu and choose **Netcaster**.

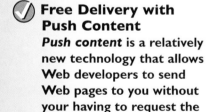

1 ▶ Click the **Start** button and choose **Programs**, **Netscape Communicator**, **Netscape Netcaster**.

2 ▶ Click the **Netcaster** tab to display the Channel Finder.

3 ▶ Click a channel button to view available pages on the channel.

4 ▶ Click **Preview Channel** to display the channel.

Next Step ▶

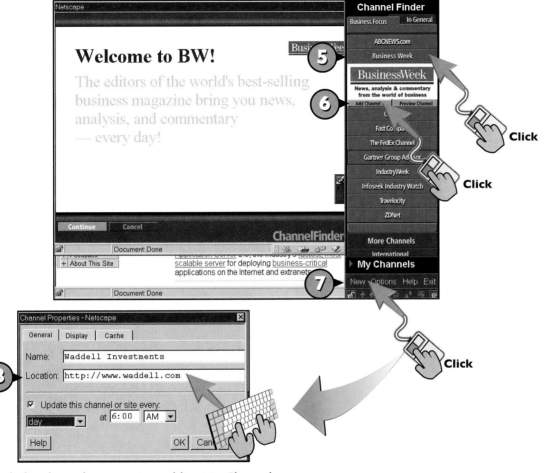

Adding a Channel

At the bottom of the Channel Finder is the My Channels button, which displays your list of Channels. You can add a channel to My Channels or add a Web page as a channel and specify how often you want updated content downloaded. To open a page you added, click My Channels and click the channel.

5 ▶ Click the channel you want to add to My Channels.

6 ▶ Click the **Add Channel** link, and follow the instructions.

7 ▶ To add a Web page as a channel, click the **New** button.

8 ▶ Enter the name, address, and desired update frequency for the page, and click **OK**.

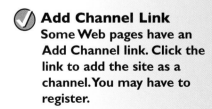 **Add Channel Link**
Some Web pages have an Add Channel link. Click the link to add the site as a channel. You may have to register.

Task 22: Tuning In with Internet Explorer Channels

Using the Channel Bar

After you install Internet Explorer 4, you have a Channel bar on your desktop, which provides access to high-quality Web sites. You can click a channel button to flip from one Web site to another.

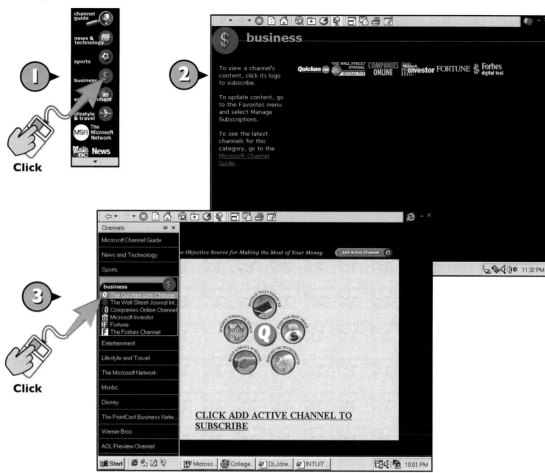

Click

Click

✓ **Channel Bar**
Click the **Channels** button in Internet Explorer's toolbar to display the Channel bar.

1 Click a channel in the Channel bar.

2 Move the mouse to the left side of the screen to bring the Channel bar into view.

3 Click the link for the desired Web page.

Adding a Channel

As you browse the Web, you may encounter pages that have an **Add Channel** link. Click the link to add the site to the **Channel bar.** You can access **Microsoft's Channel Guide** to preview additional channels and add them to the **Channel Bar.**

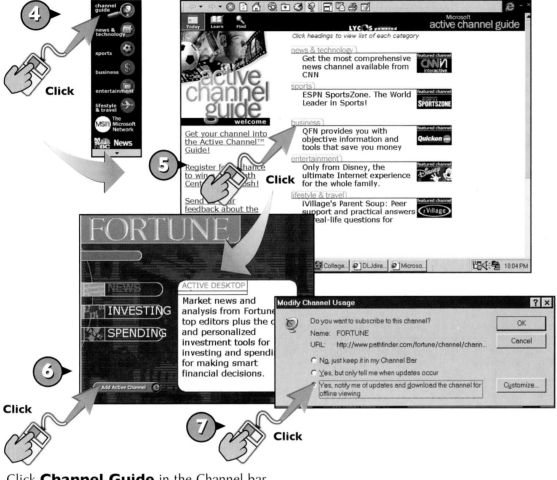

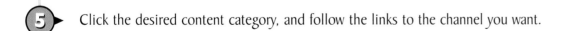

4 ▶ Click **Channel Guide** in the Channel bar.

5 ▶ Click the desired content category, and follow the links to the channel you want.

6 ▶ Click the **Add Active Channel** link.

7 ▶ Enter your subscription preferences, and click **OK**.

Task 23: Turning On the Windows Active Desktop

Viewing the Desktop as a Web Page

Internet Explorer 4 not only provides you with an excellent Web browser, but it also enhances your operating system, giving you single-click access to files on your system and integrating it with the Web. To take advantage of this desktop integration, make sure that these features are turned on.

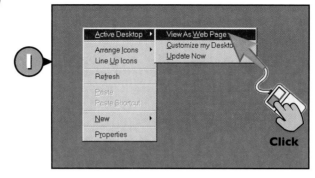

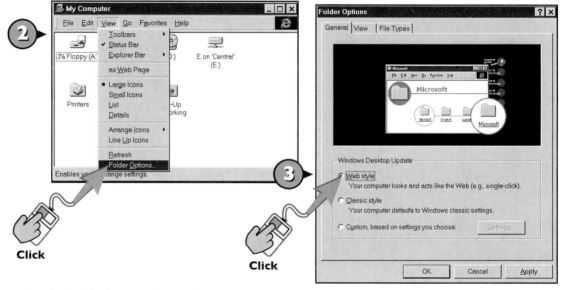

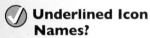 **Underlined Icon Names?**
If icon names are underlined, View as Web page is on. You now point to icons to select, and single-click to open and run.

 Single-Folder Control
You can turn off View as Web Page for individual folders in My Computer. Open the **View** menu and choose **As Web Page.**

 Right-click a blank area of your desktop, point to **Active Desktop**, and make sure **View as Web** page is checked.

 In My Computer, open the **View** menu and choose **Folder Options**.

Choose **Web Style** and click **OK**.

Task 24: Touring the Windows Active Desktop

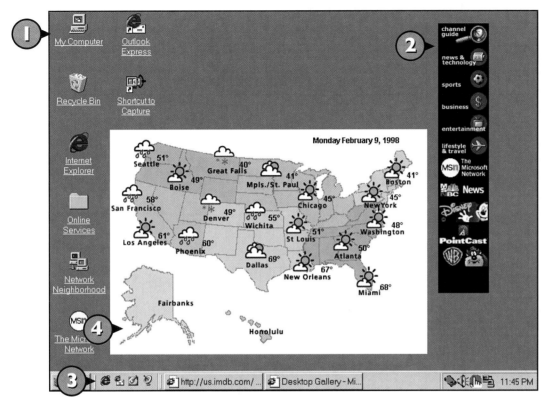

Identifying Desktop Enhancements

The Active Desktop transforms your desktop into a Webtop. Icons look and act like Web page links. The taskbar has a new toolbar, called **Quick Launch**, providing single-click access to programs. The Active Desktop also allows you to place active components, such as news tickers and weather maps, from the Web on your desktop.

✓ **Add to Quick Launch**
Drag an icon onto the Quick Launch toolbar to add it to the toolbar. Drag a folder over the toolbar to create your own toolbar.

✓ **More Toolbars**
Right-click the Quick Launch toolbar and point to **Toolbars** for additional toolbars you can turn on.

1 ▶ Icons look and act like Web page links.

2 ▶ The Channel bar lets you navigate the Web right from your desktop.

3 ▶ The Quick Launch toolbar provides single-click access to programs.

4 ▶ You can add active components to the desktop.

Task 25: Browsing the Web with Windows Explorer

Opening Web Pages in Windows Explorer

In addition to listing files and folders on your computer, Windows Explorer can now display Web pages. You simply click Internet Explorer in the folder list, and the file list window on the right displays Web pages.

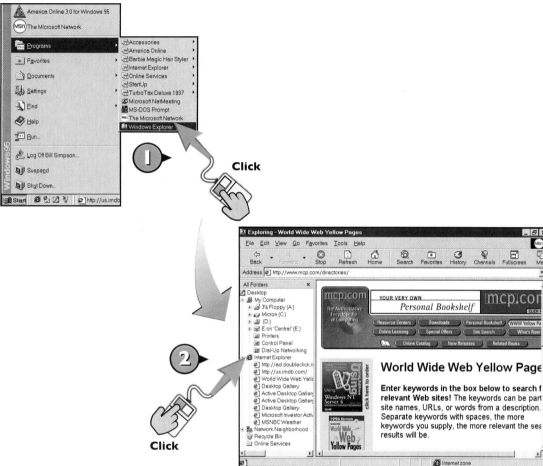

Click

Click

Code Sharing

Because Internet Explorer and Windows Explorer both support ActiveX, they can share programming code. This allows Windows Explorer to use Internet Explorer's Web navigation controls.

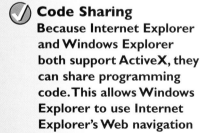 Choose **Start**, **Programs**, **Windows Explorer**.

 Scroll down the folder list, and click **Internet Explorer**.

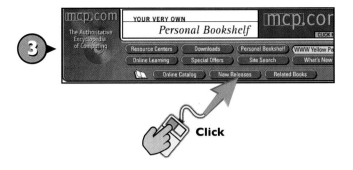

Click

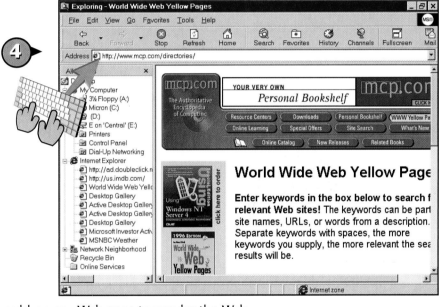

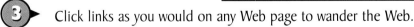

Click links as you would on any Web page to wander the Web.

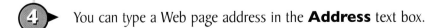

You can type a Web page address in the **Address** text box.

Task 26: Adding Active Components to the Desktop

Adding an Active Desktop Component

The Active Desktop transforms your work surface into a dynamic information center, on which you can place framed Web content, including weather maps, stock tickers, and sports score updates. These *Active Desktop components* are linked to Web sites and automatically download up-to-date information. The Channel bar is an example of an Active Desktop component, but you can install additional components.

Start Here

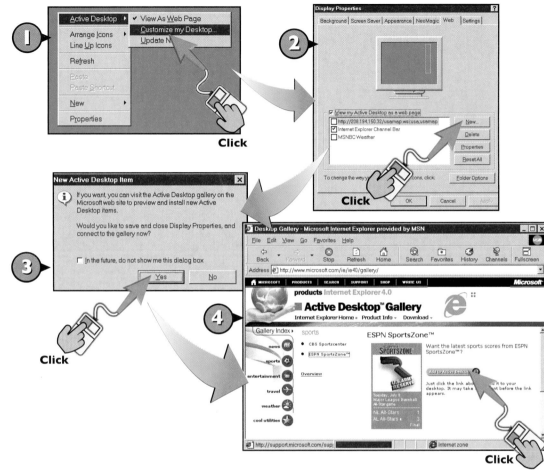

System Slowdown?
Desktop components may slow down the overall performance of Windows, especially on startup.

1 ▶ Right-click the desktop and choose **Active Desktop**, **Customize My Desktop**.

2 ▶ Click the **New** button on the Web tab.

3 ▶ Click **Yes** when prompted to go to the Active Desktop Gallery.

4 ▶ Follow the trail of links to the desired desktop component, and then click **Add to Active Desktop**.

Next Step

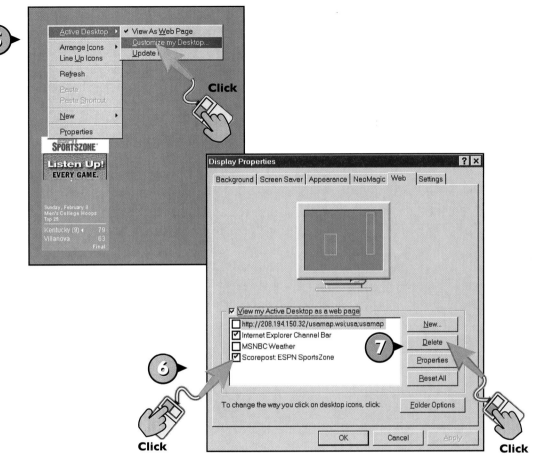

Removing a Desktop Component

If you no longer want to view desktop components, you can remove them from the desktop or completely delete them from your system.

(5) Point to the top of the component and drag the gray title bar to move the component. Right-click the desktop and choose **Active Desktop**, **Customize My Desktop**.

(6) To hide a desktop component, click its check box to remove the check mark.

(7) To remove a desktop component, click its name and click the **Delete** button.

 Web Page Desktop Backgrounds
You can use a Web page as your Windows background. Check out the Background tab.

Sending and Receiving Email Messages

Email (electronic mail) allows you to type and send a message to anyone in the world who has an Internet connection and email account. The message travels postage-free and typically arrives at its destination in a matter of seconds or minutes, rather than days. To take advantage of this free, fast delivery, you must know how to use an email program. The following tasks show you what to do.

PART

Tasks

3

PART

Task 1: Running Your Email Program

Starting Email

Internet Explorer and Netscape Communicator include their own Internet email programs: Outlook Express and Netscape Messenger, respectively. The email program connects to your Internet service provider's mail server to send and retrieve messages.

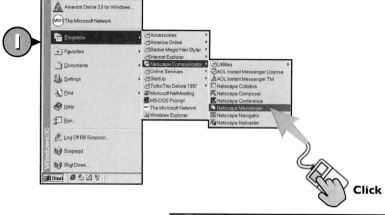

Click

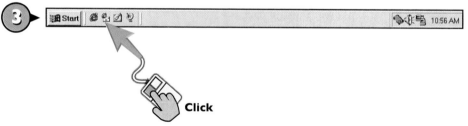

Double Click

Click

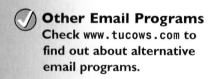

Other Email Programs
Check www.tucows.com to find out about alternative email programs.

1 To run Netscape Messenger, choose **Start**, **Programs**, **Netscape Communicator**, **Netscape Messenger**.

2 To run Outlook Express, click or double-click its icon on the desktop.

3 You can also run Outlook Express by clicking its icon in the Quick Launch toolbar.

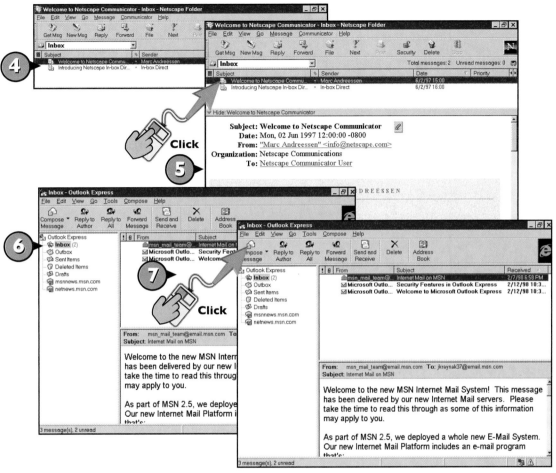

Touring the Email Screen

Although email programs all look a little different and offer different menu systems and buttons, most display a two- or three-paned window. One pane displays a list of the message descriptions, and the other displays the contents of the selected message.

(4) Netscape Messenger displays a list of messages in the upper pane.

(5) When you click a message description, the contents of the message appear in the lower pane.

(6) In Outlook Express, the left pane displays folders for incoming, outgoing, and deleted messages.

(7) Click the **Compose** or **New Message** button to write and send an email message.

✓ **Free Samples**
Most email programs come with one or two sample messages.

Task 2: Setting Up Your Email Program

Setting Up Outlook Express

Before you can send or receive email messages, you must give your email program the address of your service provider's mail server and provide your username and password (which you obtain from your ISP). You typically specify two mail servers: one for incoming mail (POP or Post Office Protocol) and one for outgoing mail (SMTP or Simplified Mail Transfer Protocol). In Outlook Express, you enter this information by creating an *email account*.

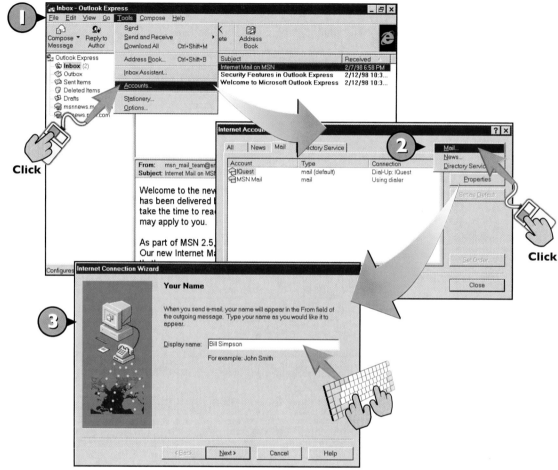

Click

Click

✓ Guess the Domain

If you know the domain name of your service provider (for example, `internet.net`), tack on "pop" or "mail" (such as `pop.internet.net` or `mail.internet.net`).

I ▸ Open the **Tools** menu and choose **Accounts**.

2 ▸ Click the **Add** button and choose **Mail**.

3 ▸ Follow the Internet Connection Wizard's instructions, and enter the required settings.

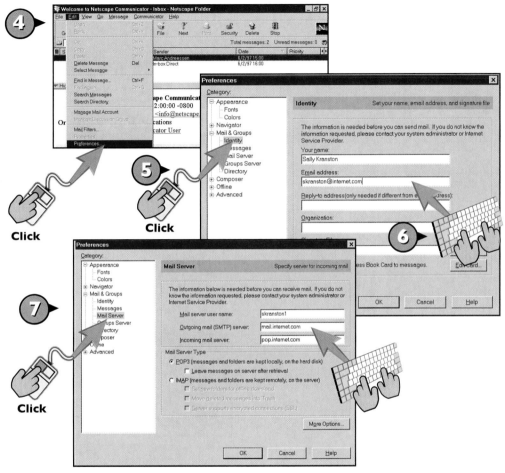

Click

Click

Click

To use Netscape Messenger to send and receive email messages, you must enter the addresses of your Internet service provider's mail servers and specify your login name. Netscape makes these options easily accessible in the Preferences dialog box.

4 ▶ Open Messenger's **Edit** menu and choose **Preferences**.

5 ▶ Under **Mail & Groups**, click **Identity**.

6 ▶ Type your name and email address.

7 ▶ Click **Mail Server**, enter your login name and your service provider's mail server addresses, and then click **OK**.

✅ **Remember Password**
You can make Messenger remember your password. Choose **Edit, Preferences,** and then click **Mail Server** under **Mail & Groups.** Click **More Options,** and turn on **Remember My Mail Password.**

End Task

Task 3: Composing and Sending Email Messages

Sending a Message

Sending a text message is a snap, assuming you know the recipient's email address. An email address consists of the person's name, nickname, or user ID followed by @, followed by the domain name of the mail server that person uses—for example, `president@whitehouse.gov`.

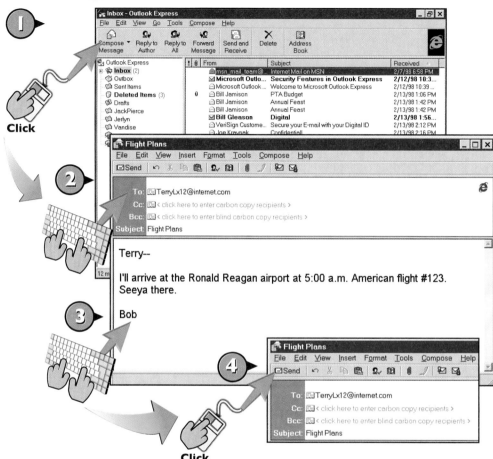

Start Here

Click

Click

 **Mass Mailing**
To send a message to more than one person, separate the email addresses with a colon and a space.

 Click the **Compose Message** or **New Message** button.

 Type the recipient's email address and brief message description in the **Subject** text.

 Click in the message area and type your message.

 Click the **Send** button.

Task 4: Sending Internet Mail from an Online Service

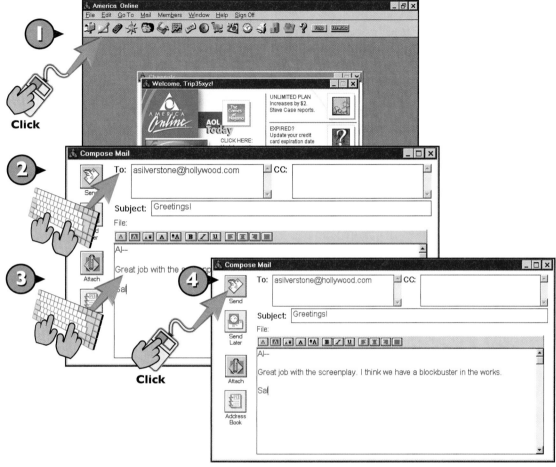

Click

Click

Sending Internet Mail

Commercial online services, such as America Online, have their own internal email system for members only. Members can address their messages to other members by using nicknames. To send an email message to a person outside of this private mail system, make sure you type the person's full Internet mail address, not just the person's name.

① Click the button for composing a new email message.

② Type the recipient's Internet email address, and then type a message description in the **Subject** text box.

③ Type your message in the message area.

④ Click the **Send** button.

✓ **Your Email Address**
If you use AOL, your Internet email address is your AOL screen name followed by @aol.com (for example, if your screen name were **Ldw Indy**, your Internet email address would be ldwindy@aol.com). You don't need to include spaces or capital letters.

End Task

Formatting Text

Email has recently graduated from simple text-based messages to include formatted text, graphics, and links. Assuming the recipient has an email program that supports **HTML** (the codes used for **Web** pages), the person can view your stylized message.

Task 5: Adding Graphics and Formatting to Messages

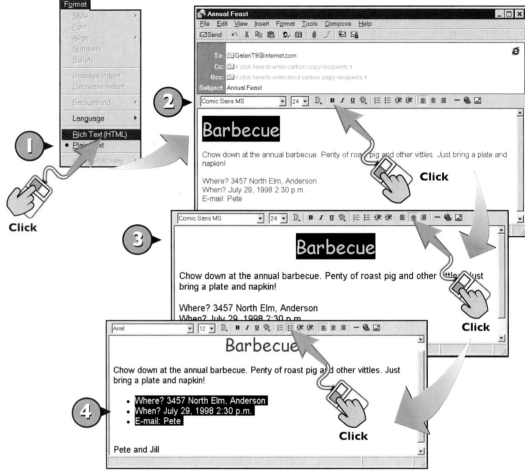

✅ **Email Stationery**
In Outlook Express, open the **Compose Message** drop-down list and choose the desired stationery. To send a plain text message, choose **Format, Plain Text.**

1 ▶ Open the **Format** menu, and choose **Rich Text**.

2 ▶ Highlight the text and click the text formatting buttons to apply the desired enhancements.

3 ▶ Click the **Center** button to center a heading or other text.

4 ▶ Use the **List** buttons to transform selected paragraphs into a numbered or bulleted list.

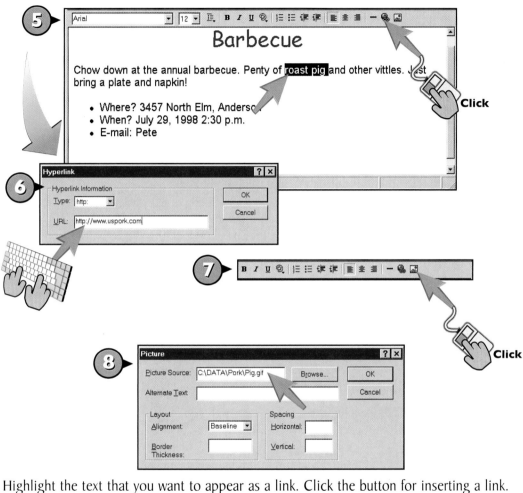

Inserting Graphics and Links

The HTML formatting toolbar also contains buttons for inserting graphics (pictures) and links that point to Web pages. The recipient can click the link to quickly open the corresponding Web page.

5 ▶ Highlight the text that you want to appear as a link. Click the button for inserting a link.

6 ▶ Type the address of the Web page you want the link to point to, and click **OK**.

7 ▶ To insert a graphic, select the option for inserting a graphic.

8 ▶ Choose the graphic file.

 Insert Object
Messenger has an Insert Object button that displays a list of objects, including links and pictures.

 End Task

Task 6: Composing Messages Offline

Writing Offline

If your Internet account charges you by the number of hours you're connected, or if you have a single phone line you use for both voice calls and the Internet, consider composing your messages offline. You can then establish your connection, send the messages, and disconnect.

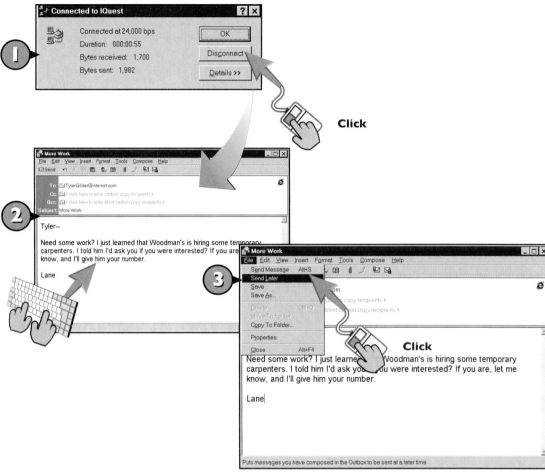

Click

Click

1. Start your email program without connecting to the Internet. If you are connected, disconnect.

2. Address and compose the message as you normally would.

3. Open the **File** menu and choose **Send Later**.

Sending Your Messages

When you choose **Send Later**, your email program places the messages in a separate folder: Outbox in Outlook Express or Unsent Messages in Messenger. You can connect to the Internet and send all the messages at once.

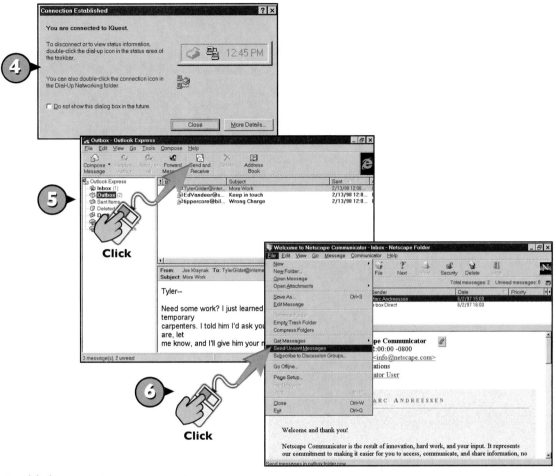

Click

Click

Establish your Internet connection.

In Outlook Express, click the **Send and Receive** button.

In Netscape Messenger, open the **File** menu and choose **Send Unsent Messages**.

 **Messenger's Unsent Messages Folder**
In Netscape Messenger, open the drop-down list just above the list of message descriptions, and choose **Unsent Messages**.

Task 7: Attaching Files to Outgoing Messages

Attaching a File

Formerly, people exchanged files by sending diskettes. Email makes the process much easier. You attach a file to your email message and send the message as you normally would. The recipient can then open the file or save it.

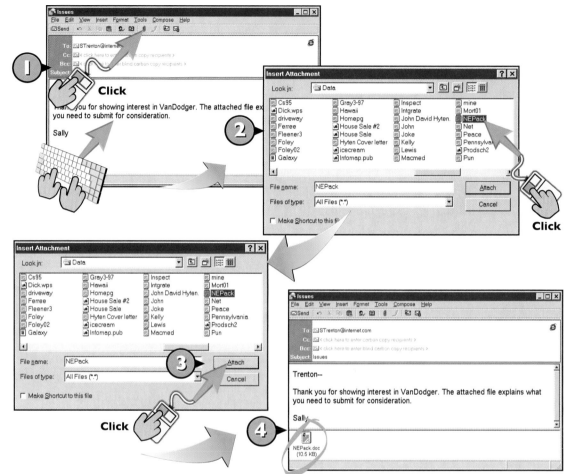

1 Compose the message as you normally do. Click the **Insert File** button, or click the **Attach** button and choose **File**.

2 Use the resulting dialog box to choose the file you want to send.

3 Click the **Attach** or **Open** button.

4 When you're done, the file or filename will appear with your message.

Next Step

Dragging and Dropping Files

You might find it easier to attach files by dragging them from a file manager window, such as My Computer, into the message area or file attachment list. This is especially useful if you have several files to attach.

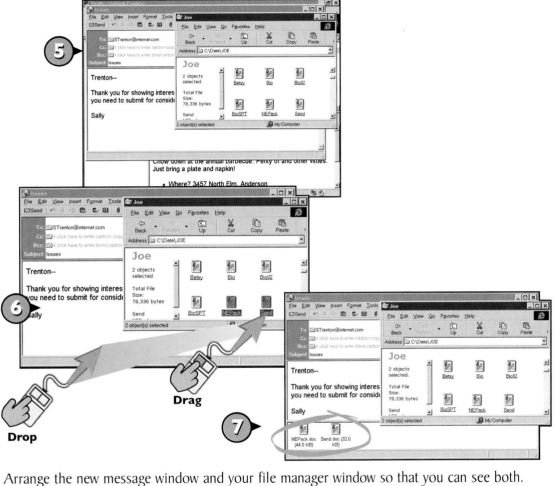

Drag

Drop

5 ▶ Arrange the new message window and your file manager window so that you can see both.

6 ▶ Drag the file you want to attach from the file manager window into the message area or file attachment list.

7 ▶ The files appear in the pane below the message area.

✓ **Attach More Files**
In Outlook Express, right-click in the attachments pane and choose **Add.**

Task 8: Using an Email Address Book

Adding Email Addresses

With an address book, you don't have to remember or type long email addresses. You just select them from a list. But first, you have to add names and email addresses to the book. The Outlook Express address book is used here as an example. To display Messenger's address book, open the **Communicator** menu and choose **Address Book.**

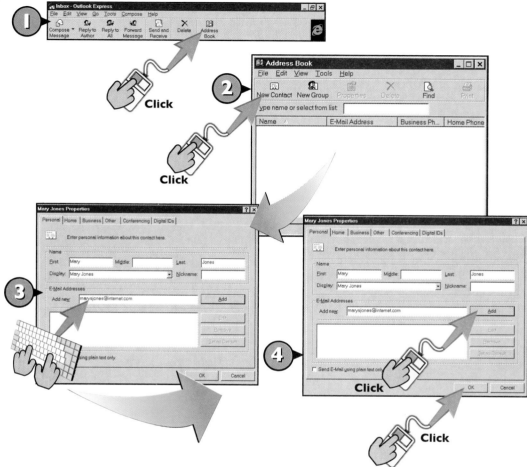

Make a Mailing List
Click the **New Group** or **New List** button and add recipients to the group.

1. Click the **Address Book** button.

2. Click the **New Contact** button.

3. Enter the person's name and email address in the appropriate text boxes.

4. Click **Add** and then click **OK**.

Next Step

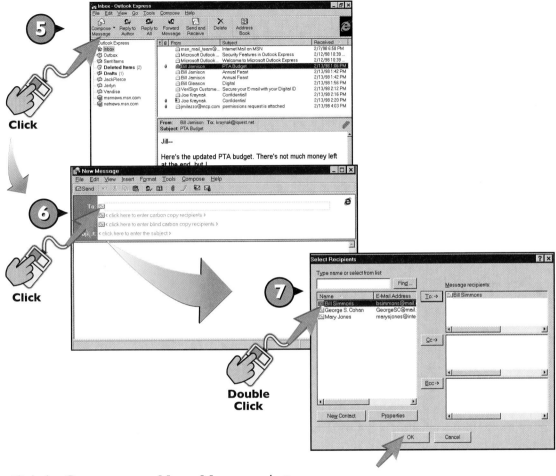

Using the Address Book

When composing a message, you can insert the recipient's email address from the address book without having to type it.

Click

Click

Double Click

5 ▶ Click the **Compose** or **New Message** button.

6 ▶ Click the card icon next to To: in Outlook Express, or click the **Address** button in Messenger.

7 ▶ Double-click the name of each person to whom you want to send the message, and then click **OK**.

✅ **Quick Addresses**
Display the message in its own window and choose **Tools, Add to Address Book (Outlook Express)** or **Message, Add to Address Book (Messenger)**.

Task 9: Reading Incoming Messages

Retrieving Messages

When someone sends you an email message, it is stored on your service provider's mail server. You use your email program to connect to the mail server, retrieve the messages, and display their contents.

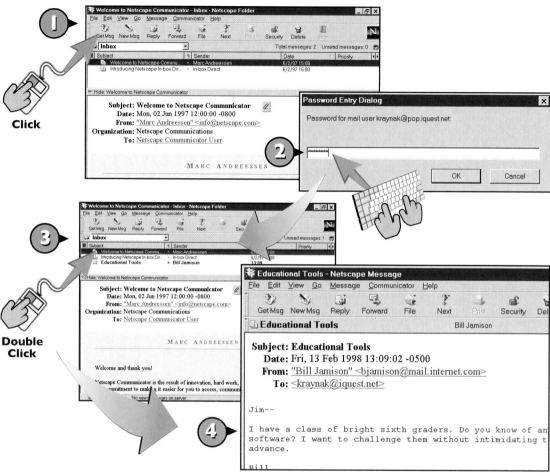

Click

Double Click

✓ **Mail Call!**
You can set up your email program to automatically retrieve incoming mail. Check your program's Options or Preferences dialog box.

① Click the **Send and Receive** or **Get Messages** button in your email program's toolbar.

② If prompted to enter your password, type your password and click **OK** (or press **Enter**).

③ If you received a message, its description appears. Double-click the message description.

④ The contents of the message appear in a separate window.

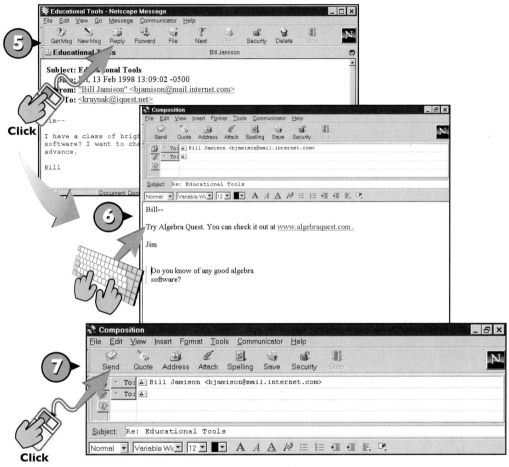

Click

Click

Replying to a Message

After you have opened a message and displayed its contents, you can quickly send a reply by clicking the **Reply** button. If the message was sent to several people, you can choose the **Reply to All** option to send your reply to everyone.

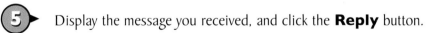

5 ▶ Display the message you received, and click the **Reply** button.

6 ▶ Type your reply, and delete as much of the quoted material as possible.

7 ▶ Click the **Send** button.

✓ **Delete Quotes**
Delete all but one or two of the quoted lines of the previous message (marked with >), so your message will require less storage space.

✓ **AOL Quotes**
To quote a message, highlight the text you want to quote before clicking the **Reply** button.

End Task

Task 10: Opening and Saving Attached Files

Opening an Attachment

Email is the most efficient way to swap files with friends and colleagues. You attach the file to your message and send it. When you receive a message with an attached file, you can quickly open the file or run it.

Virus Alert

Before opening or running an attached file, use your virus program to scan it for viruses. Don't open or run files from unknown sources.

File Associations

To open a document file by double-clicking it, the file must be associated with a program on your system. Check the Windows help system for details about file associations.

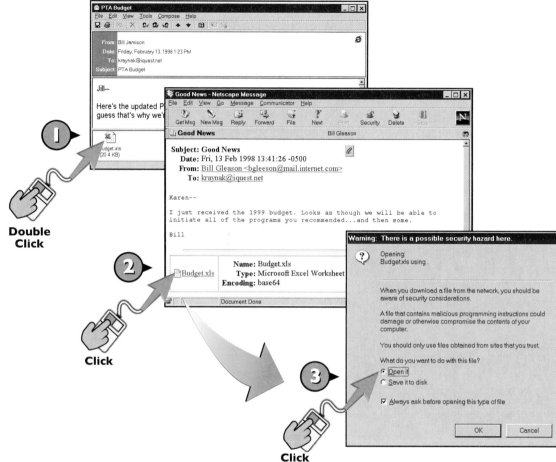

Double Click

Click

Click

 In Outlook Express, double-click the attached file's icon to open it.

 In Messenger, click the filename link at the end of the message.

 Click **Open It** and click **OK**.

Saving an Attachment

When you receive an attachment, consider saving it to your hard disk immediately. Doing so will prevent you from deleting the file by accidentally deleting the message it was attached to.

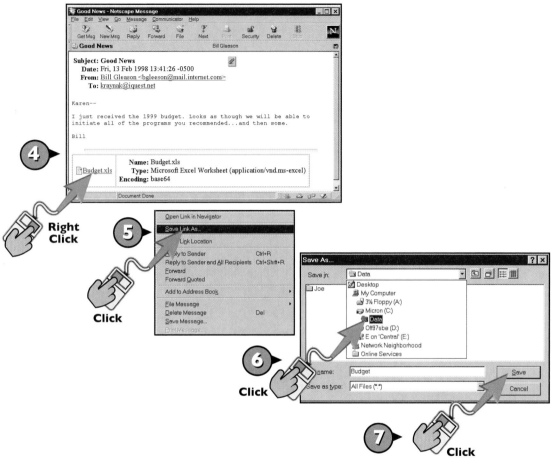

4 Right-click the attached file's icon or link.

5 Choose **Save As** or **Save Attachment As**.

6 Choose the disk and folder in which you want to save the file.

7 Click the **Save** button.

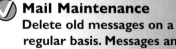

Mail Maintenance
Delete old messages on a regular basis. Messages and attachments take up space on your hard disk.

Task 11: Reading Messages Offline

Working Offline with Outlook Express

After you retrieve your messages, you don't have to stay connected to read them; they're on your hard disk. You can disconnect and read the messages at your leisure (and possibly reduce your connect-time charges). In Outlook Express, you simply choose **Work Offline**.

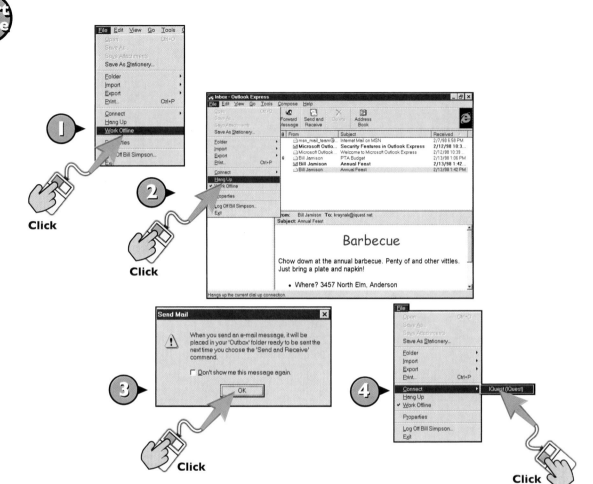

Click

Click

Click

Click

 Retrieve your messages, and then open the **File** menu and choose **Work Offline**.

 Open the **File** menu and choose **Hang Up** to disconnect. Read the messages as you normally do.

 If you try to send a message or reply, Outlook Express indicates that it will be sent to the Outbox folder. Click **OK**.

 To go back online, choose **File**, **Connect**, and click the address of your mail server.

Working Offline with Messenger

You can read messages offline in Messenger to save on connect time charges and free up your phone line. If you send a message or reply when you are offline, Messenger places it in the Unsent Messages folder. When you go back online, Messenger prompts you to send the messages.

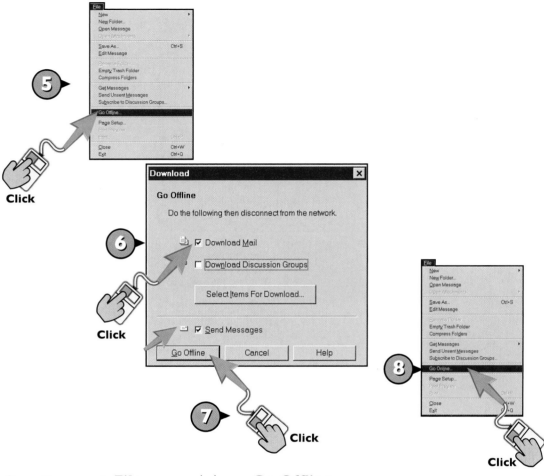

Click

Click

Click

Click

5 Open Messenger's **File** menu and choose **Go Offline**.

6 Make sure **Download Mail** and **Send Messages** are checked.

7 Click the **Go Offline** button and disconnect from the Internet.

8 To go back online, open the **File** menu and choose **Go Online**.

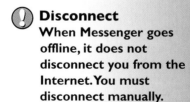

Disconnect
When Messenger goes offline, it does not disconnect you from the Internet. You must disconnect manually.

Task 12: Opening Encrypted Messages

Obtaining a Digital Certificate

To prevent people from viewing your incoming mail, you can obtain a digital certificate that provides you with a private key and a public key. You send the public key to people so they can send you encrypted messages. Your private key unscrambles the encrypted messages when you receive them.

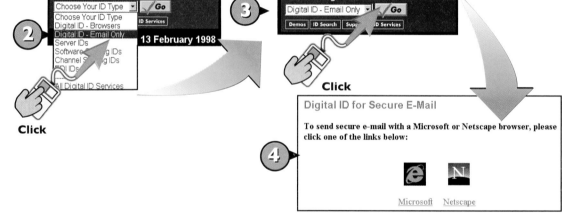

Click

Click

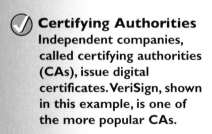

✓ **Certifying Authorities**
Independent companies, called certifying authorities (CAs), issue digital certificates. VeriSign, shown in this example, is one of the more popular CAs.

1. Use your Web browser to connect to **www.verisign.com**.

2. Open the **Choose Your ID Type** list, choose **Digital ID – Email Only**.

3. Click **Go**.

4. Follow the onscreen instructions to obtain and install your digital ID.

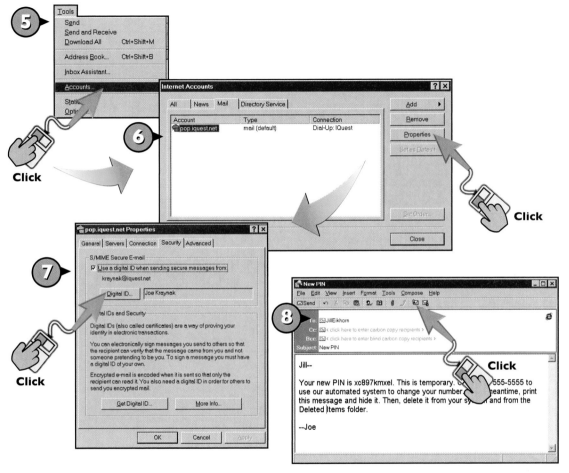

Sending Your Public Key

To enable someone to send you encrypted messages, you must send the person your public key, and the person must use the key to send you messages. These steps lead you through the process with Outlook Express.

5 ▶ Open the **Tools** menu and choose **Accounts**.

6 ▶ Click your mail server and click **Properties**.

7 ▶ On the **Security** tab, turn on **Use a Digital ID...**, click the **Digital ID** button, and choose your certificate.

8 ▶ When sending a message, click the **Digitally Sign Message** button before clicking **Send**.

 **Attach Your Public Key**
You can have your email program automatically send your public key whenever you send an email message. Check the program's security options.

 End Task

Task 13: Sending Secure Messages

Adding a Public Key to Your Address Book

If you want to send secure email messages to someone, that person must obtain a digital certificate and send you the public key for encrypting messages. You must then add the public key to the person's entry in your address book.

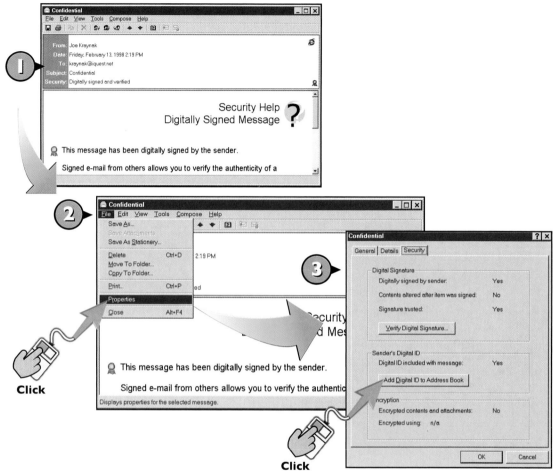

Messenger Security
Messenger keeps track of public keys for you. Click the **Security** button and click **People**.

1 ▶ Open the message that has been digitally signed.

2 ▶ Open the **File** menu and choose **Properties**.

3 ▶ Click the **Security** tab, and then click **Add Digital ID to Address Book**.

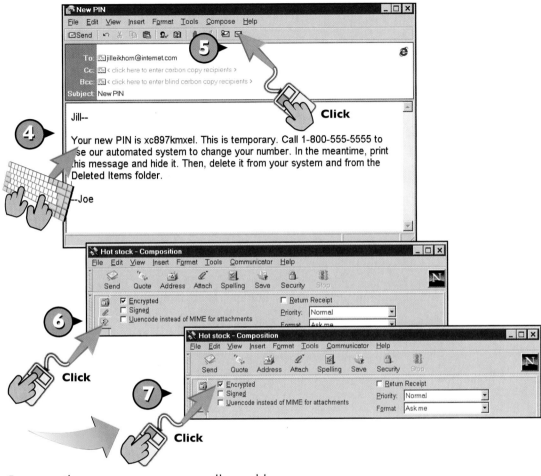

After you have added a person's public key to the address book, sending encrypted messages is easy. You compose the message as you normally would and then click an option in the New Message window for encrypting the message.

4 ▶ Compose the message as you normally would.

5 ▶ In Outlook Express, click the **Encrypt Message** button and then send your message.

6 ▶ In Messenger, click the **Message Sending Properties** tab.

7 ▶ Click **Encrypted**.

Task 14: Managing Email Messages

Creating a New Folder

As you read and reply to messages, you might not realize that they are taking up more and more hard disk space. To clean up your system, you should delete messages and place related messages you want to save in separate folders. However, you first need to create the folders.

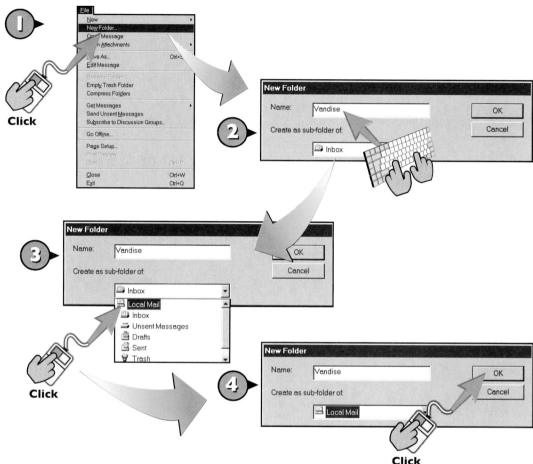

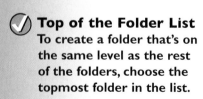

✓ Top of the Folder List
To create a folder that's on the same level as the rest of the folders, choose the topmost folder in the list.

① Open the **File** menu and choose the command for making a new folder.

② Type a name for the folder.

③ Choose the existing folder in which you want the new subfolder placed.

④ Click **OK**.

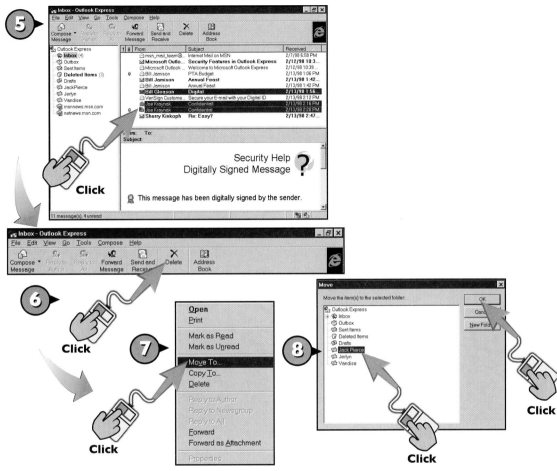

Moving and Deleting Messages

To clean up your Inbox and Sent Items folders, you can easily delete messages or move the messages to other folders in your email program. Use the same techniques to select messages as you use to select files in your file management program.

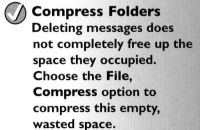

5 ▶ Highlight the names of any messages you want to delete or move.

6 ▶ To delete the selected messages, click the **Delete** button.

7 ▶ To move the messages, right-click one of the selected messages and choose **Move To** or **File Message**.

8 ▶ Select the folder to which you want the messages moved, and click **OK**.

✓ **Compress Folders**
Deleting messages does not completely free up the space they occupied. Choose the **File, Compress** option to compress this empty, wasted space.

End Task

Task 15: Filtering Email Messages

Using the Outlook Express Inbox Assistant

If you find yourself frequently moving messages from the Inbox to a different folder, consider creating a *mail filter*. The filter automatically routes incoming messages to a specific folder based on the From or Subject entries. Outlook Express features the Inbox Assistant for setting up filters.

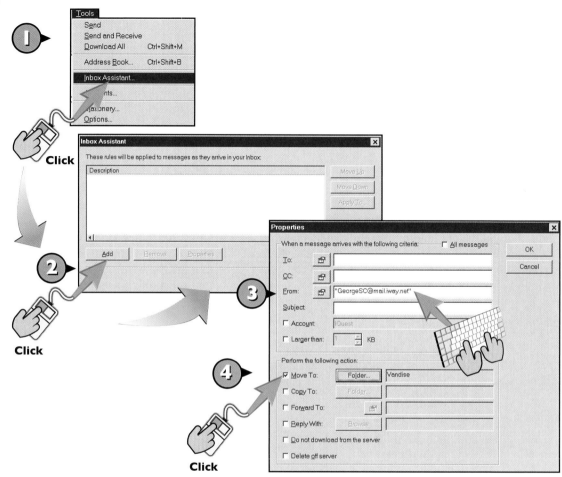

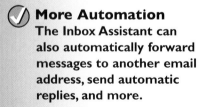

More Automation
The Inbox Assistant can also automatically forward messages to another email address, send automatic replies, and more.

1 ▶ Open the **Tools** menu, and choose **Inbox Assistant**.

2 ▶ Click the **Add** button.

3 ▶ Click in the **From** or **Subject** text box, and type an entry to specify what you want the filter to look for.

4 ▶ Click **Move To**, choose the desired folder, and click **OK**.

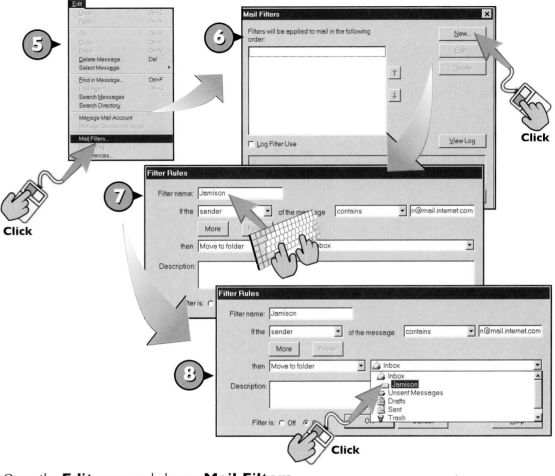

Filtering Mail in Messenger

Messenger offers a wide range of filtering options that can even route messages to specific folders based on the content of the message.

Click

Click

Click

---

5 ▶ Open the **Edit** menu and choose **Mail Filters**.

6 ▶ Click the **New** button.

7 ▶ Type a name for the filter, and enter the filter criteria.

8 ▶ Choose the folder to which you want messages that meet the specified criteria moved, and click **OK**.

More Options
Look through all the drop-down lists before entering your options.

End
Task

Page
93

4

Reading and Posting Newsgroup Messages

Newsgroups (commonly called discussion groups or Usenet) are electronic message boards, where users post messages for all to see. Over 20,000 public newsgroups cover topics from politics to body piercing to computer issues. To read newsgroup postings and post your own messages, questions, and replies, you must be able to use a **newsreader**. The following tasks show you what to do:

Tasks

Task 1: Running Your Newsreader

Running Outlook Express

Internet Explorer includes its own Internet newsreader, called Outlook Express, which you can use for email, as well. The newsreader connects to your Internet service provider's news server to give you access to newsgroups.

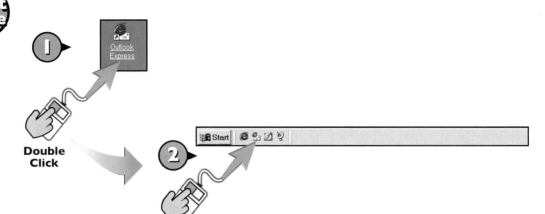

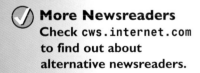

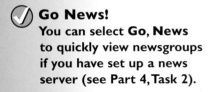

To run Outlook Express, double-click its icon on the desktop.

You can also run Outlook Express by clicking its icon in the Quick Launch toolbar.

Outlook Express may prompt you to connect to a news server (see Part 4, Task 2).

Running Netscape Collabra

Netscape Communicator's newsreader is called Netscape Collabra. It shares many features with Messenger, the email program, so if you use Messenger, making the transition to Collabra will be easy.

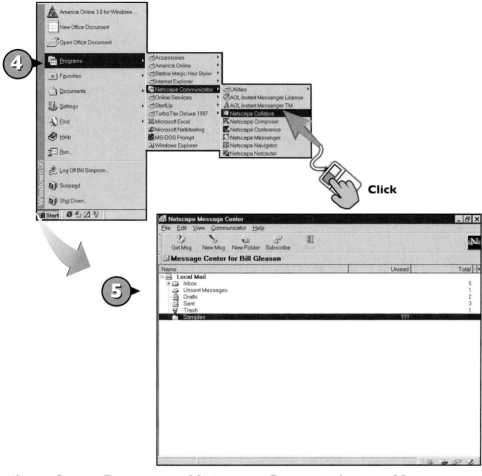

Click

④ Choose **Start**, **Programs**, **Netscape Communicator**, **Netscape Collabra**.

⑤ The Message Center appears (see Part 4, Task 2).

✓ **Navigator->Collabra**
Press **Ctrl+3** to run Collabra from **Navigator** or **Messenger**.

✓ **Component Bar**
Choose **Communicator**, **Show Component Bar** to display a toolbar that lets you quickly run the Communicator programs.

Task 2: Setting Up Your Newsreader

Task 2: Setting Up Your Newsreader

Setting Up Outlook Express

Before you can access newsgroups, you must give your newsreader the address of your service provider's news server (NNTP) and provide your username and password (if required). In Outlook Express, you enter this information by creating a news account.

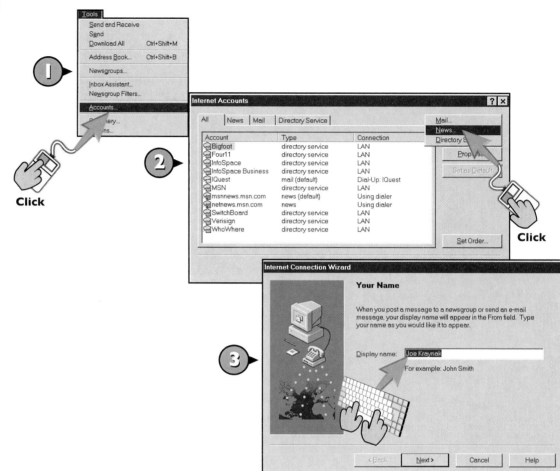

Click

Click

✅ Guess Your News Domain

The news server address typically consists of "news" or "nntp" followed by your ISP's domain name (for example, news.internet.com).

 Open the **Tools** menu and choose **Accounts**.

 Click the **Add** button and choose **News**.

 Follow the Internet Connection Wizard's instructions, and enter the required settings.

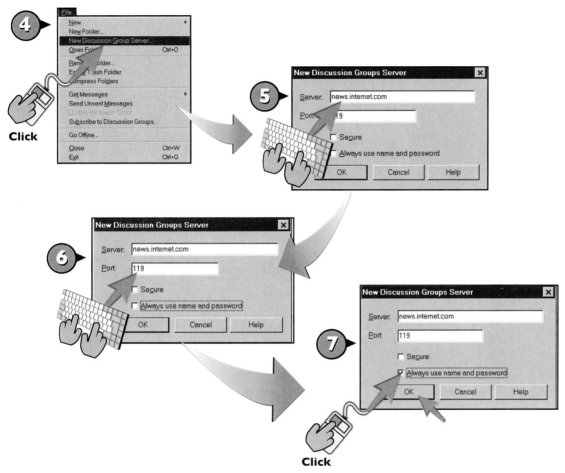

Setting Up Netscape Collabra

To access newsgroups with Netscape Collabra, you must enter the addresses of your Internet service provider's news server and specify any login information, if required.

Click

Click

④ In the Message Center window, open the **File** menu and choose **New Discussion Group Server**.

⑤ In the Server text box, type the address of your service provider's news server.

⑥ If your service provider specified a port number, enter it.

⑦ If you need to enter your name to log on to the server, choose **Always Use Name and Password**. Click **OK**.

 More Options
Choose **Edit, Preferences,** and click the plus sign next to **Mail & Groups** for additional discussion group options.

End Task

Going to Newsgroups

Commercial online services have their own forums and message boards, but most services allow you to access Internet newsgroups as well. Here, you learn how to access newsgroups from America Online.

Task 3: Accessing Newsgroups from a Commercial Online Service

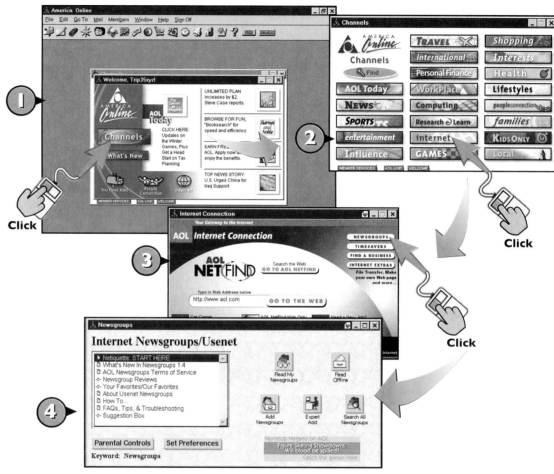

Click

Click

Click

Click

✅ **Keyword Newsgroups**
Press **Ctrl+K**, type newsgroups, and click **Go**.

✅ **Clunky Newsreader**
America Online's newsreader is clunky. Establish your AOL connection, and then use a different newsreader.

1 Connect to America Online, and click the **Channels** button.

2 Click the **Internet** button.

3 Click **Newsgroups**.

4 The Newsgroups window appears, displaying buttons for viewing newsgroups.

Making a Short List of Newsgroups

The best way to view newsgroup messages is to *subscribe* to the newsgroup to add it to a short list of newsgroups that interest you. You can then view the list of messages posted to subscribed newsgroups.

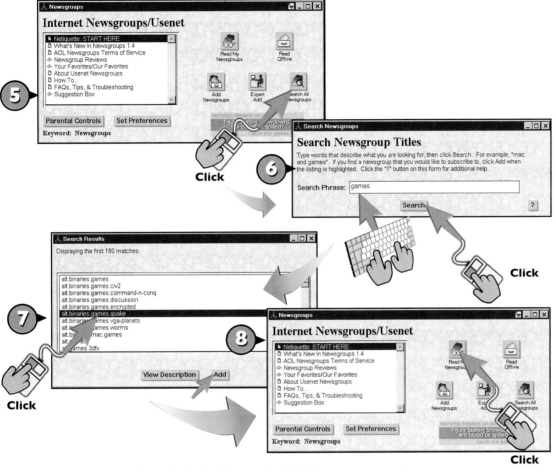

Click

Click

Click

Click

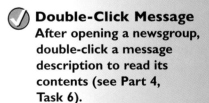

5 In the Newsgroups window, click the **Search All Newsgroups** button.

6 Type a word that describes the desired topic, and click **Search**.

7 Click the desired newsgroup, click **Add**, and click **OK**.

8 Return to the Newsgroups window, and click **Read My Newsgroups**.

✓ **Double-Click Message**
After opening a newsgroup, double-click a message description to read its contents (see Part 4, Task 6).

Downloading Newsgroup Names

Your ISP's news server contains the names of thousands of newsgroups. You must connect to the news server and download the list of newsgroups to determine what is available.

✓ **Get Newsgroups on Startup**
If your newsreader prompts you to download or subscribe to newsgroups when you set up a news server, give your okay.

⚠ **Patience**
It can take several minutes for your newsreader to download the newsgroup list, so be patient.

Task 4: Downloading and Finding Newsgroups

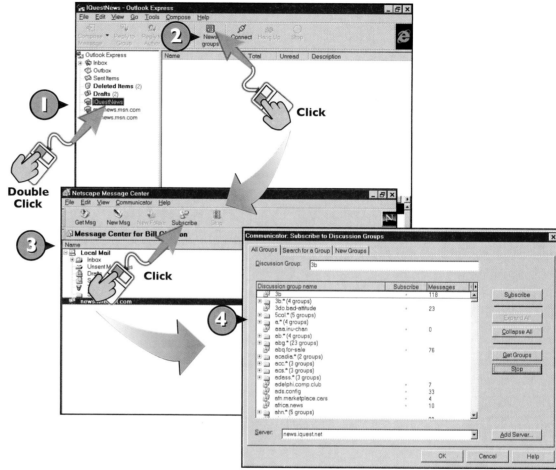

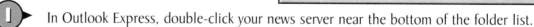

1 ▶ In Outlook Express, double-click your news server near the bottom of the folder list.

2 ▶ Click the **News Groups** button.

3 ▶ In Collabra, click the **Subscribe** button.

4 ▶ Your newsreader downloads the list of newsgroups and displays them.

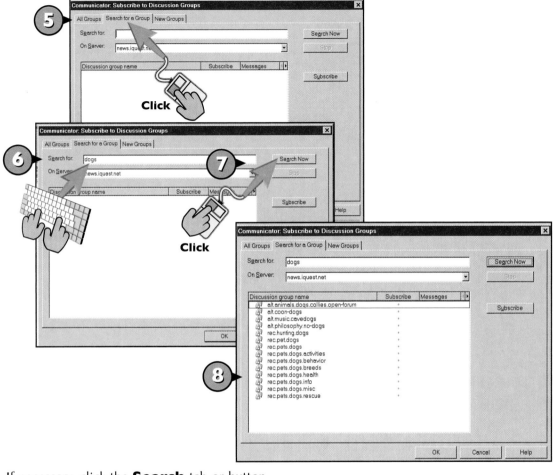

Searching for Newsgroups

Because newsgroup lists are so long, newsreaders offer tools to help filter the list. You enter a word or string of characters that specifies your interest, and the newsreader displays a short list of newsgroup names that match your entry.

5 ▶ If necessary, click the **Search** tab or button.

6 ▶ In the text box above the newsgroup list, type a word that describes your interest.

7 ▶ If necessary, click the **Search** button.

8 ▶ The newsreader displays names of only the newsgroups that match your entry.

PART

Subscribing to Newsgroups

Subscribing to a newsgroup places it on a short list of newsgroups, making it easier for you to find the newsgroup later and read recent postings.

Task 5: Subscribing to Newsgroups

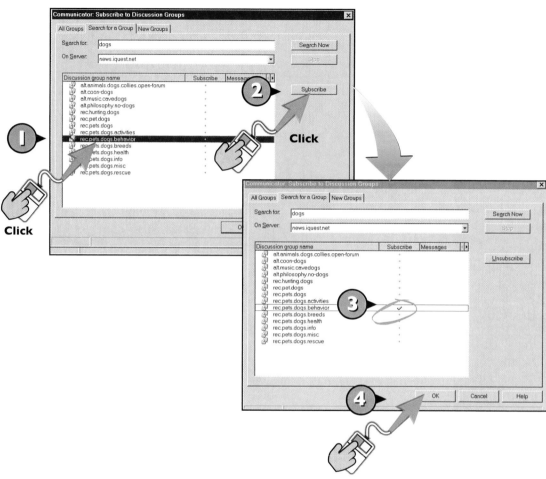

Click

Click

Click

✅ **Quick Subscription**
In Collabra, click the dot in the Subscribed column to subscribe to the newsgroup.

✅ **Double-Click to Subscribe**
In Outlook Express, double-click the newsgroup's name to subscribe to it.

① Click the name of the newsgroup that you want to add to your subscription list.

② Click the **Subscribe** button.

③ Your newsreader marks the newsgroup with a special icon.

④ Click **OK**.

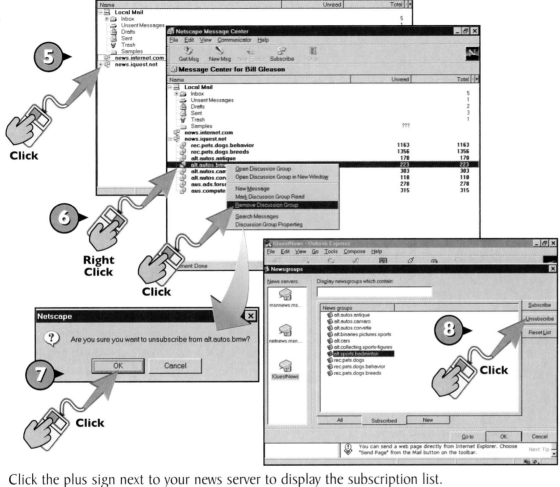

If you lose interest in a newsgroup, you should remove the newsgroup from your list of subscribed newsgroups. This prevents the newsreader from automatically downloading message descriptions for new postings.

5 Click the plus sign next to your news server to display the subscription list.

6 Right-click the newsgroup's name and choose the option for canceling the subscription or removing the discussion group.

7 Click **Yes** or **OK** to confirm.

8 You can also unsubscribe in the Newsgroups window.

End Task

Task 6: Reading Newsgroup Messages

Displaying the Contents of a Message

After subscribing to a newsgroup, you can pull up a list of messages that other people have posted. Your newsreader displays a list of message descriptions. To read a message, you just click its description.

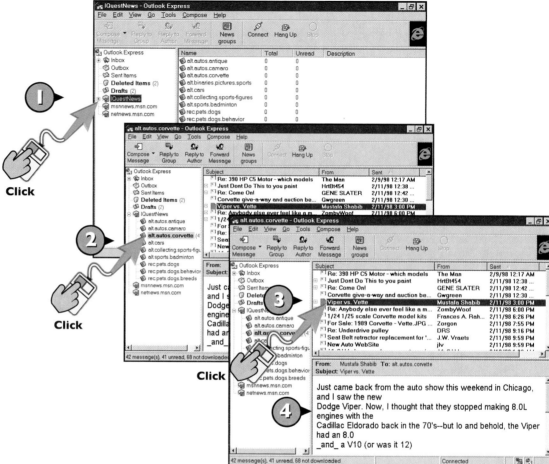

Start Here

Click

Click

Click

✅ **Message Window**
Double-click the message description to display the message in its own window.

✅ **More Messages**
Your newsreader may download a limited number of message descriptions. Specify the desired number in the **Options** or **Preferences** dialog box.

1 ▶ Click the plus sign next to your news server's name, if necessary.

2 ▶ Click or double-click the newsgroup's name.

3 ▶ Click the description of the message you want to read.

4 ▶ The contents of the message appear below the message list.

Next Step

Following a Discussion Thread

When someone posts a message, others may post replies to that message. Your newsreader groups the original message and replies, so you can follow the *thread* of the conversation.

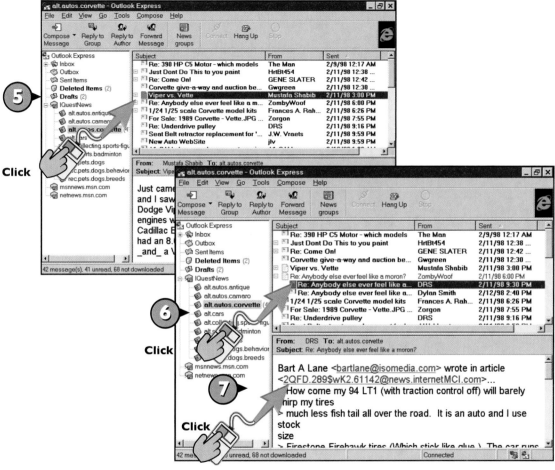

Click

Click

Click

(5) Click the plus sign next to the original message.

(6) Click the description of the message that appears below the original message.

(7) The contents of the reply appear in the pane below the message list.

Scattered Threads
If messages and their replies are not grouped, check the thread option on your **View, Sort** menu.

Navigate Message Window
If the message is displayed in its own window, click the **Next Message** button to scroll through messages.

Task 7: Replying to a Posted Message

Post Your Reply Publicly

As you read posted messages, you will feel compelled to reply to the author. You can do this by posting your reply in the newsgroup, where everyone can read it, or by sending your reply privately with an email message. Here, you learn how to post a reply to the newsgroup.

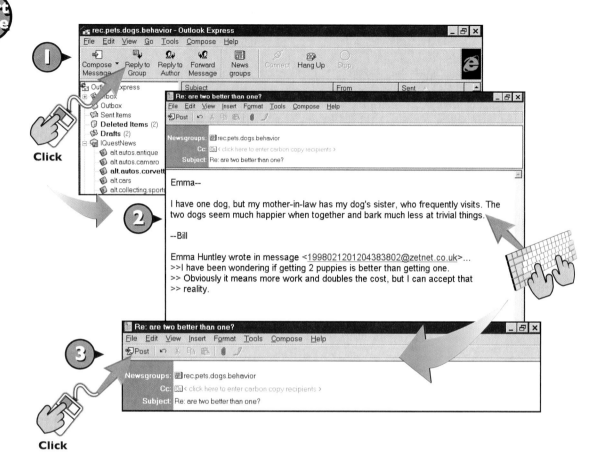

Start Here

Click

Click

✓ **Check Back Later**
Your reply will not immediately pop up in the newsgroup. Check for it later.

✓ **Collabra Replies**
The Reply button in Collabra opens a drop-down list containing options for replying publicly or privately.

With the message you want to reply to selected, click the **Reply to Group** button.

Type your reply in the message area, and delete any unnecessary lines quoted from the original message.

Click the **Post** or **Send** button.

Reply Privately Via Email

Many people request that you send a reply via email instead of posting it publicly. This ensures some privacy in addition to saving the person the time it takes to check the newsgroup for replies. When you choose to reply privately, your newsreader uses your email program to send the reply.

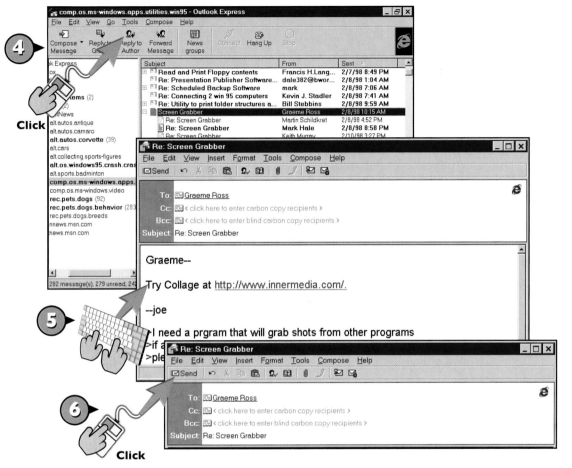

Click

Click

4 ▶ With the message you want to reply to selected, click the **Reply to Author** button.

5 ▶ Type your reply in the message area, and delete any unnecessary lines quoted from the original message.

6 ▶ Click the **Send** button.

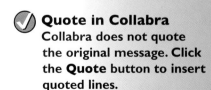 **Quote in Collabra**
Collabra does not quote the original message. Click the **Quote** button to insert quoted lines.

Task 8: Starting Your Own Discussion

Following Newsgroup Etiquette

Newsgroups are essentially Internet communities, and people are proud of the communities in which they live. When you post a message or reply, be polite, don't verbally attack anyone, and follow the newsgroup code of conduct.

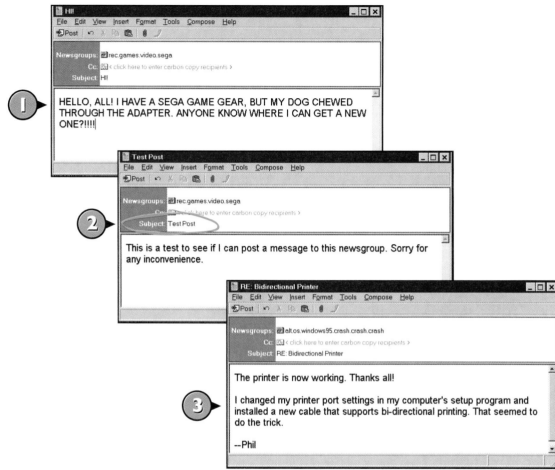

Spamming
Although you can post the same message to every newsgroup, don't. This constitutes spamming and is frowned upon by all.

1. Typing in all uppercase is the equivalent of shouting. DON'T DO IT.

2. If you post a test message, type **Test** or **Ignore** in the **Subject** text box.

3. If you request private replies, post a reply to your original message summarizing the replies. (Keep it short.)

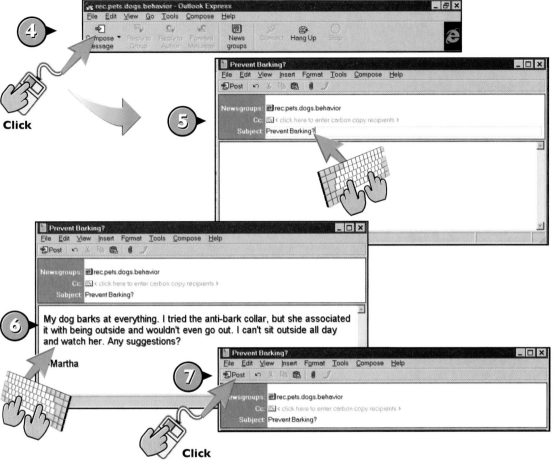

Posting a New Message

You can start your own discussion by posting a message to a newsgroup. When you post a message, anyone who accesses the newsgroup can view your message and reply to it. If you want replies sent by email, be sure to add your request.

4 Choose the desired newsgroup, and click the **Compose Message** or **New Msg** button.

5 Type a clear description of your message in the **Subject** text box.

6 Type the contents of your message.

7 Click the **Send** or **Post** button.

 Keep It Short
Keep your messages brief, and post them only to newsgroups in which the content of your message applies.

PART 4

Task 9: Working with Attached Files

Opening and Saving Attached Files

In some newsgroups, users commonly post files. You might find graphics files in a photography or fine arts newsgroup or game enhancements in a computer game newsgroup. You can open these files or save them to your disk. (Most attached files are images embedded in the message.)

Virus Alert

Attached files may contain computer viruses. Scan the file for viruses before running or opening it. Try the shareware version of McAfee VirusScan, which you can obtain from www.nai.com.

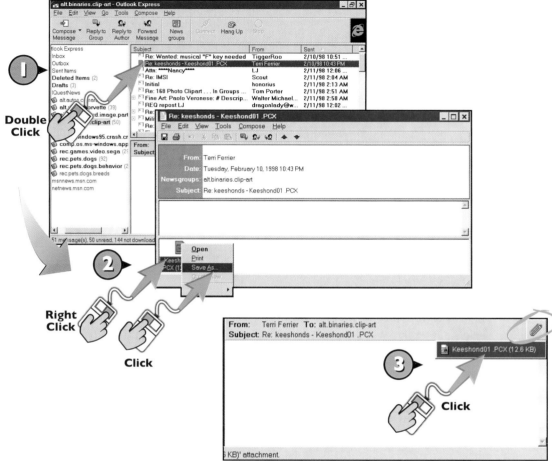

Double Click

Right Click

Click

Click

1 ▶ Double-click the message that contains the attached file.

2 ▶ Right-click the file's link or the image, and choose the **Save** or **Open** option.

3 ▶ In Outlook Express, click the paperclip icon, and click the file's name to open it.

Next Step

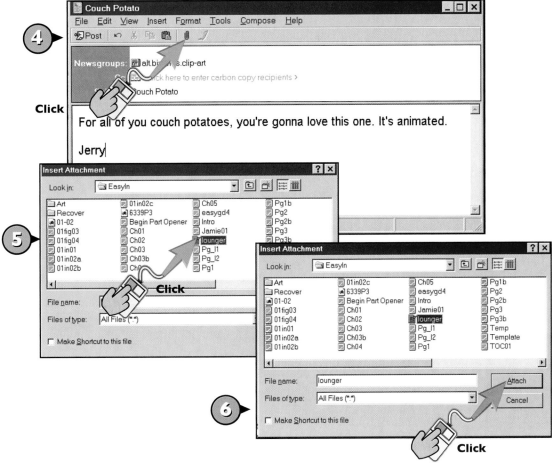

Sending Attached Files

If you connect to a newsgroup in which users commonly post files, you can share a file with others by attaching it to a message.

(4) Compose the message as you normally do. Click the **Insert File** button, or click the **Attach** button and choose **File**.

(5) Use the resulting dialog box to choose the file you want to send.

(6) Click the **Attach** or **Open** button.

✅ **Embedded Graphics**
You can also insert graphics right inside your message (see Part 3, Task 5).

✅ **Drag-and-Drop Attachments**
Drag a file from your file manager into the message area to quickly attach it.

End Task

Going Offline with Outlook Express

Outlook Express can download message descriptions or descriptions and message contents. You can then disconnect from the Internet and read the messages at your leisure.

Task 10: Reading Newsgroup Messages Offline

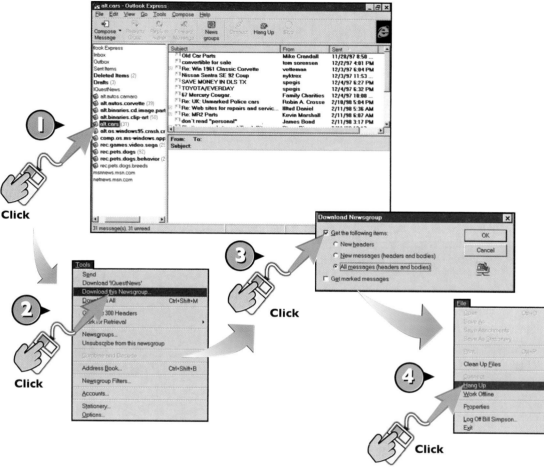

①▸ Click the name of the newsgroup you want to read offline.

②▸ Open the **Tools** menu, and choose **Download This Newsgroup**.

③▸ Click **Get the Following Items,** and choose the items you want. Click **OK**.

④▸ Open the **File** menu and choose **Hang Up**.

Next Step

Going Offline with Collabra

You can read messages offline in **Collabra** to save on connect time charges and free up your phone line. If you send a message or reply when you are offline, **Collabra** places it in the **Unsent Messages** folder. When you go back online, **Collabra** prompts you to send the messages.

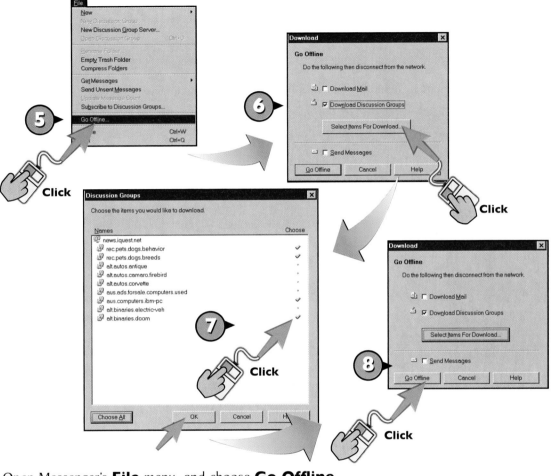

Click

Click

Click

Click

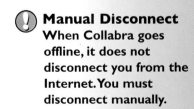

⑤ Open Messenger's **File** menu, and choose **Go Offline**.

⑥ Make sure **Download Discussion Groups** is checked and click **Select Items for Download**.

⑦ Click the dot next to each newsgroup you want to download, and click **OK**.

⑧ Click the **Go Offline** button.

Manual Disconnect
When Collabra goes offline, it does not disconnect you from the Internet. You must disconnect manually.

End Task

Downloading (Copying) Files from the Internet

Many Internet sites act as huge hard disk drives, called FTP servers, from which you can download (copy) free programs, shareware programs (try before you buy), games, video clips, and other fun and useful files. To download files from an FTP server, you must be able to connect to and navigate the server. The following tasks provide a visual tour to quickly bring you up to speed.

Tasks

Task 1: Understanding FTP

FTP Servers

FTP (short for *File Transfer Protocol*) is a language that computers use to transfer files across the Internet. There are thousands of FTP servers around the world from which you can download (copy) files to your computer.

Start Here

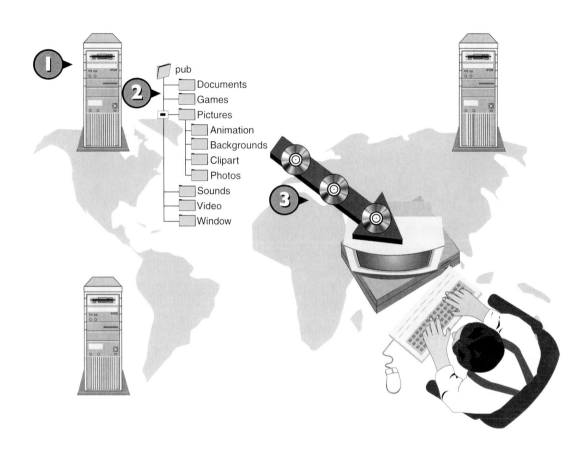

Virus Check

Most FTP sites check their files regularly for viruses. However, before running or opening a downloaded file, you should check it using an antivirus program. Try the shareware version of McAfee VirusScan, which you can obtain from **www.nai.com**.

1 ▶ FTP servers are like huge hard disks that you can access with your Internet connection.

2 ▶ The files are stored in folders called *directories* on the FTP server.

3 ▶ Using your Web browser or an FTP program, you can copy files from the FTP server to your hard disk drive.

Public and Private FTP

FTP servers come in two flavors: public (also called *anonymous*) and private. You can connect to public FTP servers by entering a generic username, such as *guest*, and using your email address as your password. Private FTP servers require a secret password to connect.

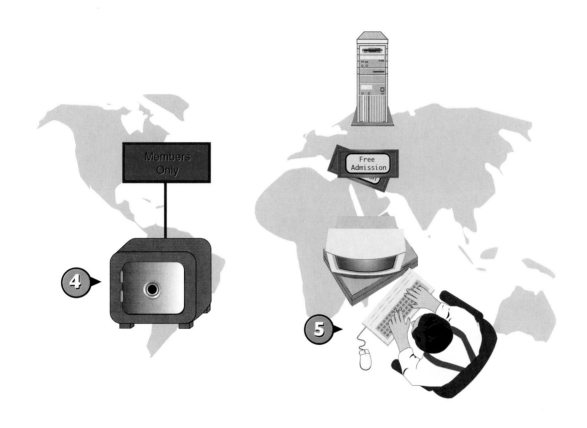

 Private FTP servers are like private clubs. Without the right password, your admittance is denied.

 Public FTP servers let anyone connect and copy files by logging in as a guest.

 Busy Signals
Public FTP servers are typically busy. You'll have better luck connecting during the late evening and early morning.

Finding Programs on the Web

Most casual Internet users use **FTP** to get programs that they want to try out. But wandering through FTP servers and directories is no way to search. A better way is to connect to Web sites dedicated to helping users find useful files.

Task 2: Finding Shareware Programs

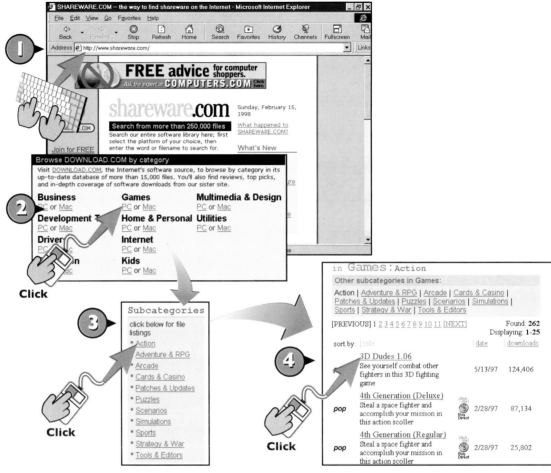

✓ **Shareware Sites**
You can find some popular shareware sites at
cws.internet.com
www.tucows.com
www.bsoftware.com
www.jumbo.com
www.winsite.com

1 ▶ Use your Web browser to connect to CINET's shareware site at **www.shareware.com**.

2 ▶ Scroll down the page, and click the link for your system type in the desired software category.

3 ▶ Click the link for the desired subcategory.

4 ▶ You'll find plenty of links and reviews to keep you busy for hours.

Finding Files with Archie

In some cases, you may find the file you want, but the server is too busy to send it to you. In such cases, jot down the name of the file, and use an **Archie** search page on the Web to find a different server that has it. (Popular FTP sites have clones, called **mirror sites**.)

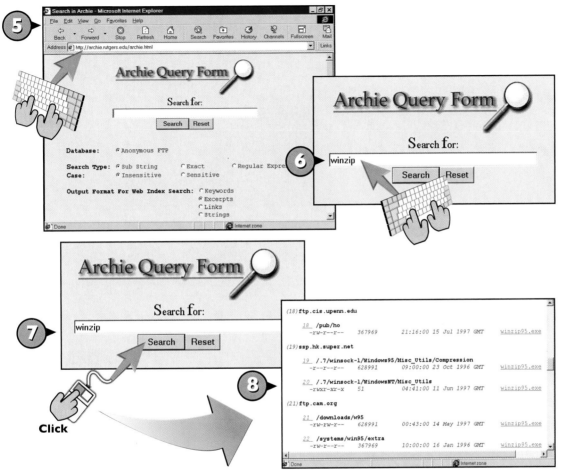

Use your Web browser to connect to **archie.rutgers.edu/archie.html**.

Type the name (or partial name) of the file you're looking for.

Click the **Search** button.

If Archie finds the file, it displays links for downloading it.

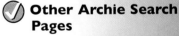 **Other Archie Search Pages**
www.thegroup.net/AA.html
cuiwww.unige.ch/archieplex form.html
www.ucc.ie/cgi-bin/archie

Search Yahoo!
Search for "shareware" or the name of the program you're looking for.

Downloading from a Web Page

Most Web browsers, including Internet Explorer and Netscape Navigator, support FTP. The easiest way to download files is to click the button for downloading the file or right-click the file's link and choose the **Save** option.

Task 3: Downloading a File with Your Web Browser

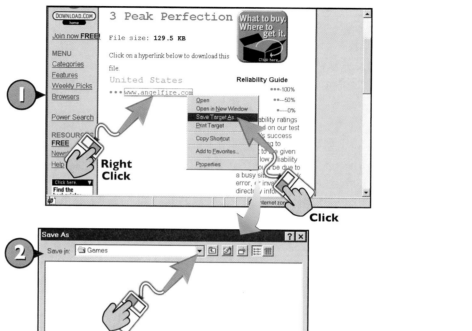

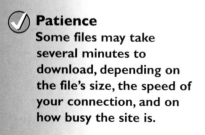

✓ Patience
Some files may take several minutes to download, depending on the file's size, the speed of your connection, and on how busy the site is.

1 ▶ If you encounter a link that points to a file, right-click the link and choose **Save File As** or **Save Target As**.

2 ▶ Use the resulting dialog box to choose the folder in which you want to save the file.

3 ▶ Click the **Save** or **OK** button.

4 ▶ A dialog box appears, showing the download progress.

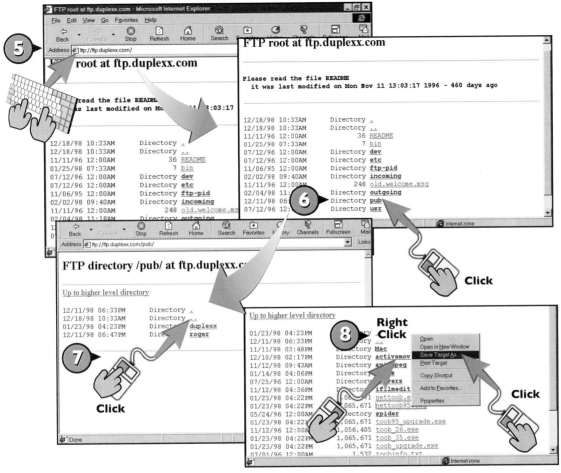

Downloading from an FTP Site

Downloading from the Web is much like navigating a Web page—you simply click a link. An FTP site is a little different, because you must switch from one folder to another; it's more like navigating your hard drive.

⑤▶ Enter the address of the FTP site, starting with **ftp://**.

⑥▶ A list of directories appears. Click the link for the desired directory, typically the **/pub** directory.

⑦▶ You can click the **Back** button to return to the previous list, or click the pair of dots to move back up.

⑧▶ When you see a file you want, right-click its link and choose **Save File As** or **Save Link As**.

✓ README.TXT
Many sites have a README.TXT link. Click it, and read the resulting text file to learn more about the site.

Downloading and Installing CuteFTP

Although your Web browser provides an easy way to download files, its speed cannot compare to that of a genuine FTP program. One of the best FTP programs around is CuteFTP, which is fast, in addition to being easy to use.

Task 4: Downloading and Installing an FTP Program

Start Here

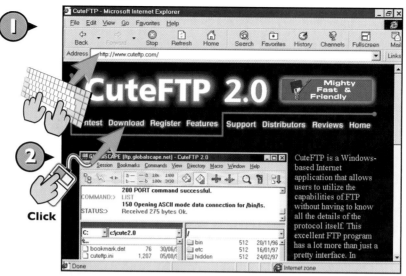

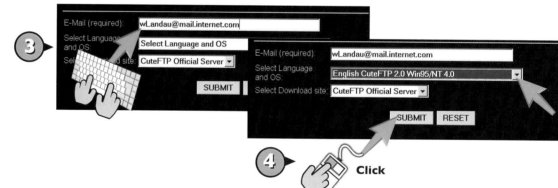

① Steer your Web browser to **www.cuteftp.com**.

② Click the **Download** link.

③ Scroll down the page, and enter your email address.

④ Choose your operating system from the drop-down list, and click **Submit**.

Next Step

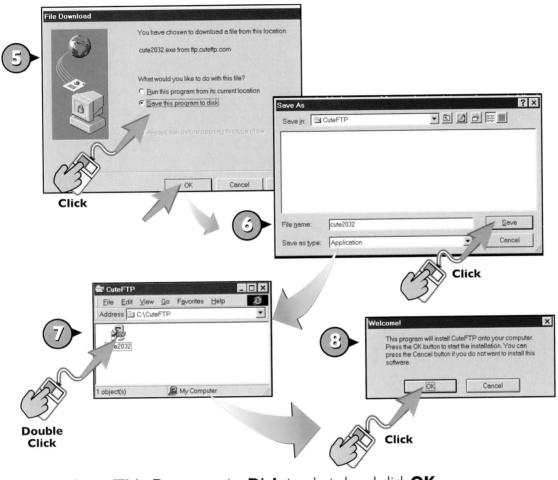

Click

Click

**Double
Click**

Click

 Make sure **Save This Program to Disk** is selected, and click **OK**.

 Choose the disk and folder in which you want the file saved, and click the **Save** button.

 When the download is complete, open the folder where the file is stored, and double-click the file.

 Follow the onscreen instructions to complete the installation.

 Other FTP Programs
Check out other FTP
programs at
cws.internet.com or
www.tucows.com.

PART

Task 5: Connecting to an FTP Server

Connecting to a Listed Server

CuteFTP and most other FTP programs come with a list of FTP servers you can connect to. You select the desired server from the list, and the FTP program connects to the server and enters your email address as the password.

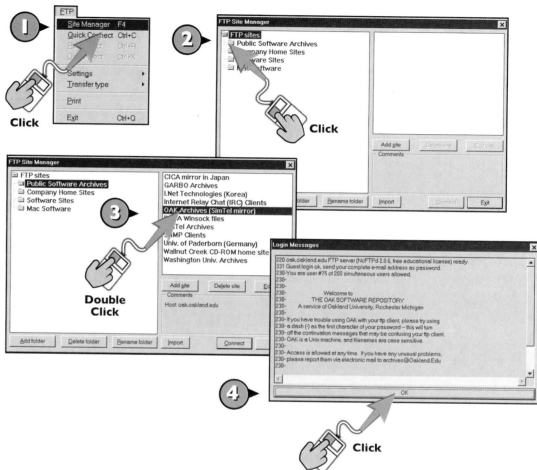

✓ **Disconnected?**
The login screen displays the connection status. If a server is busy, you may not connect.

✓ **Index Too Long**
If you receive a message indicating that the index file is too long, choose to skip the process of downloading the index file.

① Open the **FTP** menu and choose **Site Manager**.

② Click the folder for the desired site type.

③ Double-click the name of the desired FTP server.

④ CuteFTP connects you to the server and displays the login screen. Click **OK**.

Next Step

Adding an FTP Site

If the FTP server you want to connect to is not listed, you must enter the server's address. If you need to connect to a private FTP server, you must also enter your username and password.

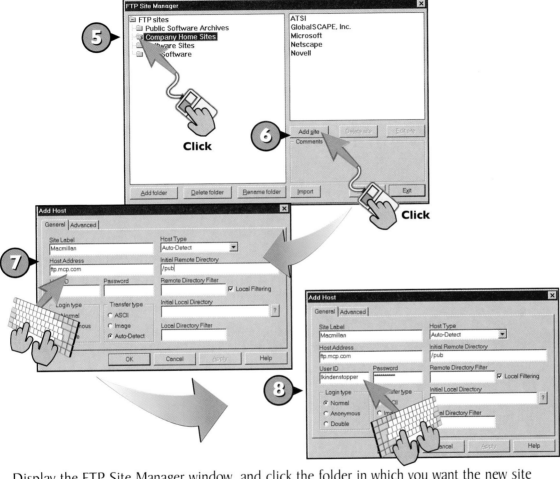

Click

Click

5 Display the FTP Site Manager window, and click the folder in which you want the new site placed.

6 Click the **Add Site** button.

7 Type the site's name, address, and starting directory (if required).

8 To connect to a private FTP server, enter your login name and password. Click **OK**.

Changing Directories

When you connect to an
FTP server, your FTP
program displays the
contents of your system in
one panel and the contents
of the FTP server in
another panel. Before
copying files, you must open
the **destination** folder on
your computer and the
source directory (folder)
on the FTP server.

Task 6: Downloading Files Using an FTP Program

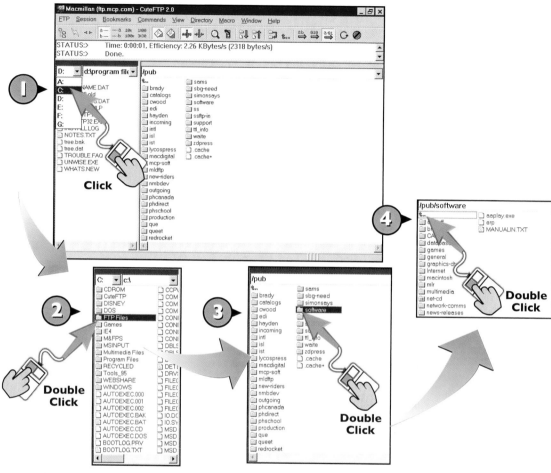

Click

Double Click

Double Click

Double Click

✓ **Go to /pub**
Most public servers have a
directory named /pub,
where you will find the
most commonly
downloaded files.

1 Open the **Drive** drop-down list, and choose the desired disk drive on your computer.

2 Double-click the folder in which you want to store the downloaded file.

3 Double-click a folder in the FTP server directory list to open it.

4 Double-click the arrow at the top of the list to move up to the previous directory.

Copying Files

After you have located the desired file, copying it is easy. You drag the file from the FTP server panel into the panel that displays the destination folder (on your disk). It's just like copying files in any file management program.

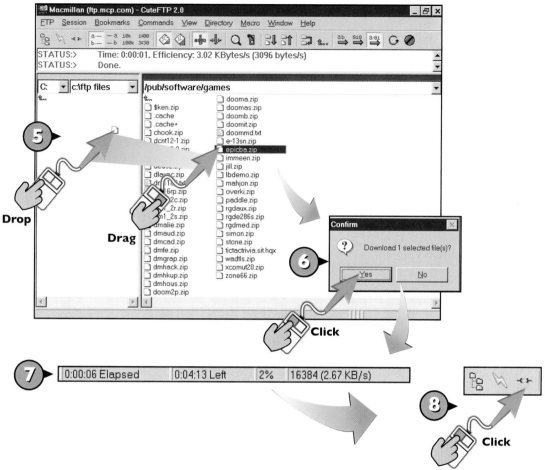

Drop

Drag

Click

Click

5 ▸ Drag the file from the FTP server panel into the panel that displays the open folder on your computer.

6 ▸ When prompted to confirm, click **Yes**.

7 ▸ The status bar displays the progress of the download.

8 ▸ When you are done, click the **Disconnect** button.

Be Quick About It
As a courtesy to other users, stay connected to the FTP server only long enough to download the desired file. Download files during off-hours, if possible.

End Task

Downloading WinZip

Many files at FTP sites are compressed to minimize the storage space required and decrease download time. To decompress a file (*extract* its contents), you need a special tool called a *compression* utility. Here, you learn how to download a popular compression utility for Windows, called WinZip.

Task 7: Downloading and Installing a Compression Utility

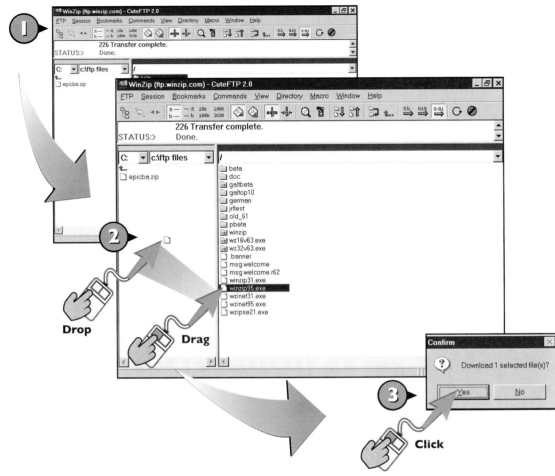

Drop

Drag

Click

Confirm
Download 1 selected file(s)?
Yes   No

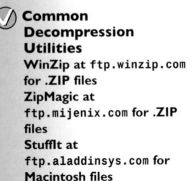

✅ **Common Decompression Utilities**
WinZip at `ftp.winzip.com` for **.ZIP** files
ZipMagic at `ftp.mijenix.com` for **.ZIP** files
StuffIt at `ftp.aladdinsys.com` for Macintosh files

1 Use your FTP program to connect to `ftp.winzip.com`.

2 Drag the desired file (winzip95.exe for Windows 95) from the FTP server pane into the pane for your open folder.

3 Click **Yes**.

Next Step

Installing a File Compressor

The decompression program you downloaded is stored as a self-extracting file, meaning that it can decompress itself. Just double-click the file, and follow the onscreen instructions.

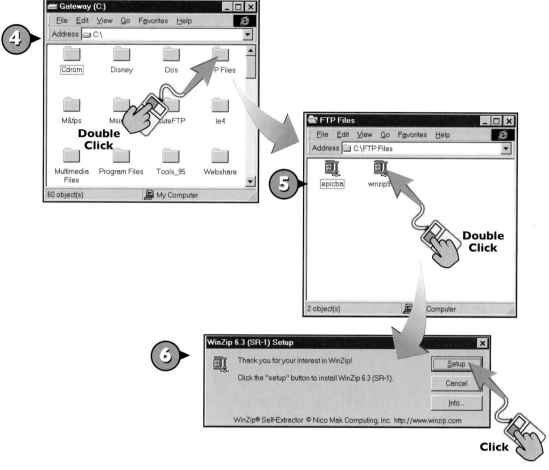

4 Change to the folder to which you downloaded winzip95.exe.

5 Double-click **winzip95.exe**.

6 Follow the onscreen instructions to complete the installation.

✓ Compressed File Formats
Compressed PC files are commonly stored in the ZIP format. Compressed Macintosh files are typically stored as **HQX, SIT,** or **BIN.** Other common file types include **ARC, ARJ,** and **GZ.**

Task 8: Decompressing Compressed Files

Decompressing a File

After downloading a compressed file, you can double-click the file to open it in WinZip and then extract its contents. (Some compressed files have more than one file inside.) To use other decompression programs, you may have to drag the file into the compression utility's window.

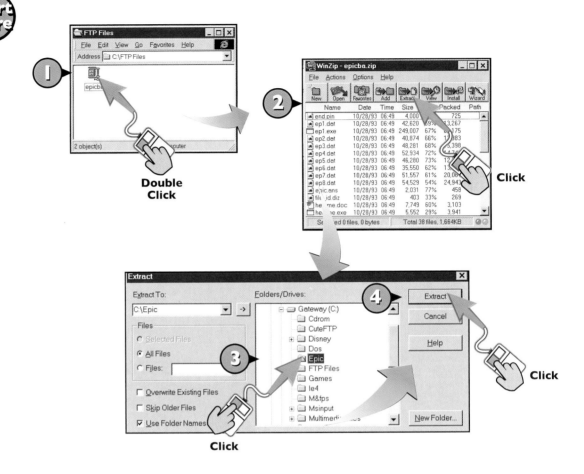

Double Click

Click

Click

Click

✓ **Open a File**
To open or run a file without extracting it first, double-click its name in the WinZip window.

① ▶ Double-click the compressed file.

② ▶ Click the **Extract** button.

③ ▶ Choose the disk and folder in which you want the extracted file(s) placed.

④ ▶ Click the **Extract** button.

Task 9: Installing Downloaded Programs

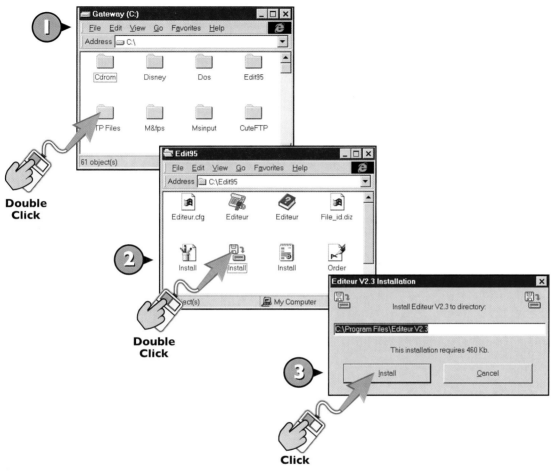

Double Click

Double Click

Click

Installing a Program

Most programs you download are packaged as self-extracting files. To install the program, you double-click the file you downloaded and follow the onscreen instructions as you do with any program. In some cases, however, you must decompress the file and then run the installation.

 Change to the folder to which you extracted the program's files.

 Double-click the **Setup** or **Install** file.

 Follow the onscreen installation instructions.

 No Setup or Install File?
You may have to run the program by clicking its executable file, commonly a file whose name ends in .exe or .bat.

Chatting on the Internet

Twenty-four hours a day, seven days a week, you will find people chatting on the Web—meeting in virtual rooms and carrying on conversations by typing on the screen. With your Internet connection and your Web browser or a special chat program, you can explore the world of online chat and meet people from all over the world.

Tasks

Task 1: Chatting on the Web

Chatting at Yahoo!

In addition to offering one of the more popular Web search tools, Yahoo! plays host to thousands of chatters every day. Because Yahoo! offers a Java-based chat program (*client*), all you need to start chatting is your Web browser.

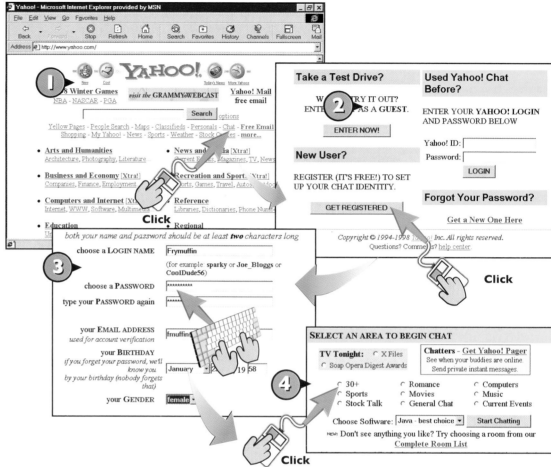

Start Here

Click

Click

Click

1 ▶ Open Yahoo!'s home page at **www.yahoo.com**, and click the **Chat** link.

2 ▶ Scroll down the page, and click the **GET REGISTERED** button.

3 ▶ Follow the onscreen instructions to register, and enter a name to identify you.

4 ▶ Under Select an Area to Begin Chat, select the desired chat topic or area.

Next Step

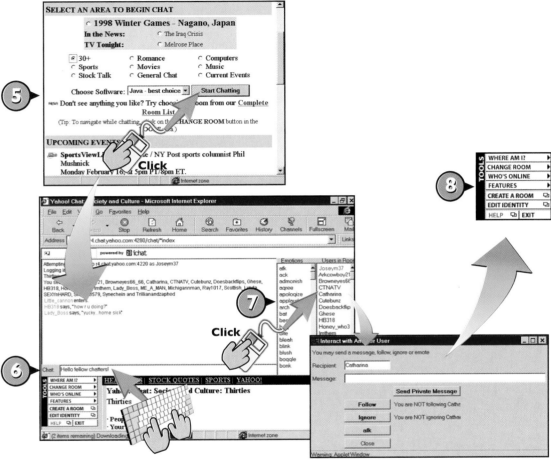

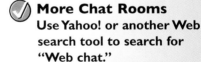

More Web Chat

You can find additional places to chat on the Web that use plug-ins, ActiveX controls, and even forms to enable you to chat with your browser. Check out the following:

www.hotwired.com/talk
www.worldvillage.com/wv/chat/html/chat2.htm
www.chatplanet.com

5 Click the **Start Chatting** button.

6 Type your message in the text box below the running discussion, and press **Enter**.

7 Click a chatter's name to find out about the person or send the person a private message.

8 Use the chat area tools to get help, change rooms, edit your identity, find out who's chatting where, and more.

More Chat Rooms
Use Yahoo! or another Web search tool to search for "Web chat."

Task 2: Chatting with Microsoft Chat

Chatting in a Comic Strip

Internet Explorer comes with a chat program, called Microsoft Chat, that lets you take on the persona of a comic strip character. In addition to chatting with typed messages, your character can gesture to other people.

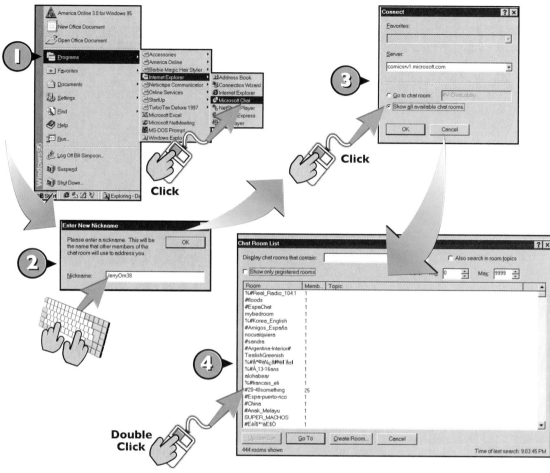

Click

Click

Double Click

✓ **No Microsoft Chat?**
If you don't have Microsoft Chat, open Internet Explorer's **Help** menu and choose **Product Updates**. If you're using Netscape Navigator, you can download Microsoft Chat from www.microsoft.com/ie/chat.

1 ▶ Choose **Start**, **Programs**, **Internet Explorer**, **Microsoft Chat**.

2 ▶ Type a name to identify yourself in chat rooms, and click **OK**.

3 ▶ Choose **Show All Available Chat Rooms,** and click **OK**.

4 ▶ Double-click the name of the desired room.

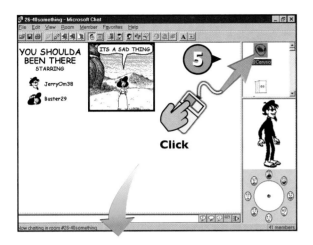

Click

Additional Options

Microsoft Chat is packed with features too numerous to cover in a few steps. Check out the menus and button bars for additional options. You can pick a different character, enter a description of yourself, pick different chat scenes, create your own room, and much more. Check out the Help system for details.

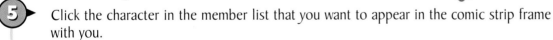

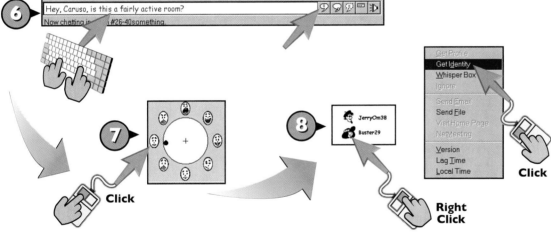

Click

Right Click

Click

5 ▶ Click the character in the member list that you want to appear in the comic strip frame with you.

6 ▶ Type your message in the message text box, and click **Say**.

7 ▶ To change your character's posture or facial expression, click an expression in the **Emotion Wheel**.

8 ▶ To view personal information about someone in the chat room, right-click the person's character and choose **Get Identity**.

✓ **No Comic Strip**
To turn off the comic strip, open the **View** menu and choose **Plain Text**.

End Task

Downloading an IRC Program

Although Web chat is becoming more popular, you'll find more people chatting with specialized chat programs to access **IRC (Internet Relay Chat)**. Here's a list of some of the better chat programs and where you can get them:
mIRC at `www.mirc.com`
Visual IRC at
`virc.melnibone.org`
PIRCH page at
`www.bcpl.lib.md.us/~frap pa/pirch.html`

IRC Primer
You'll find plenty of useful information about IRC at the mIRC home page.

Task 3: Downloading and Installing an IRC Program

Start Here

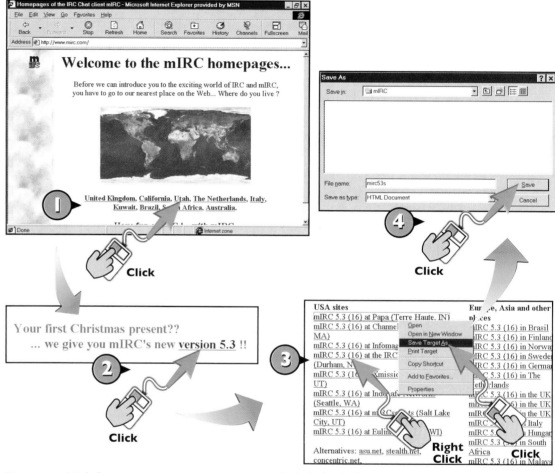

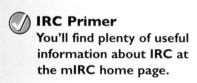

1. Steer your Web browser to **www.mirc.com**, and click the link to an mIRC page near you.

2. Click the link for downloading the latest version of mIRC.

3. Scroll down the page, right-click the link for a download site near you, and choose the **Save Target As** option.

4. Use the resulting dialog box to save the file to a folder on your hard disk.

Installing the IRC Program

To use your new IRC program, you must install it. mIRC comes as a self-extracting, self-installing program file. You double-click the file and follow the onscreen instructions to install it.

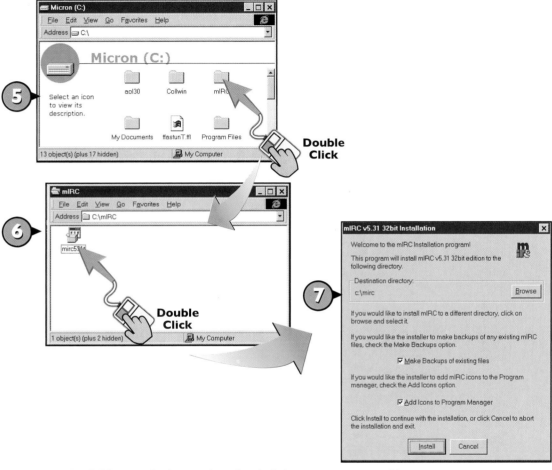

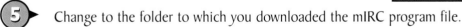

Change to the folder to which you downloaded the mIRC program file.

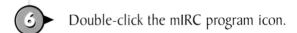

Double-click the mIRC program icon.

Follow the onscreen installation instructions.

Task 4: Logging On to a Chat Server and Picking a Room

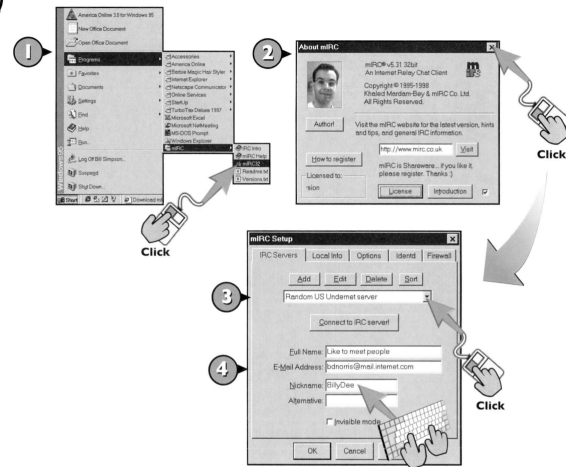

Choosing a Chat Server in mIRC

Before you can chat, you must connect to a chat server (a computer on the Internet specialized for handling IRC). The chat server is connected to other chat servers to make a network (such as EFnet or Undernet), giving you the opportunity to chat with thousands of people around the world.

Start Here

Click

Click

Click

Click

✓ **Remember to Pay**
mIRC is a shareware program, so you can try it before paying for it. If you keep using it, register and pay for the program.

✓ **Real Name?**
Instead of typing your real name in the Full Name text box, type a comment you want people to see when they check you out.

1 Choose **Start**, **Programs**, **mIRC**, **mIRC32**.

2 Click the **Close** button to close the Introduction window.

3 Open the chat server drop-down list, and choose one of the Random server entries.

4 Type your name, email address, and a name to identify you in chat rooms.

Next Step

Picking a Room

When you are connected to a chat server, a list of chat rooms (also called *channels*) appears. Choose the desired room. You can leave rooms, enter other rooms, and even chat in several rooms at the same time (although following the discussions is tough).

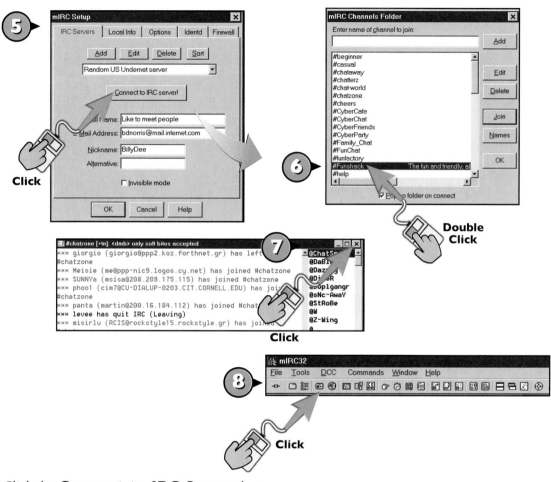

Click

Double Click

Click

Click

(5) Click the **Connect to IRC Server** button.

(6) In the list of available rooms, double-click the desired room.

(7) To exit a room, click the window's **Close** button.

(8) To pick a different room, click the **Channels Folder** button, and double-click the room name.

✓ **Start Your Own Room**
In the mIRC Channels Folder window, type a name for your room, and click the **Add** button.

Task 5: Chatting in a Room or Channel

Chatting in Public

Connecting to a chat server and finding a room that interests you are the most difficult aspects of chatting. When you're in a chat room, sending messages is easy. You type your message in a text box and press **Enter**.

1 ▶ Whenever anyone in the room sends a message, it pops up in the discussion pane.

2 ▶ Type your message in the message area, and press **Enter**.

3 ▶ Your message appears in the discussion pane and on the screens of everyone else in the chat room.

Next Step

Checking Out the Other Chatters

As you chat, you might become curious about a person in the room and want to find out more about that person. If the person created a profile, you can check it out.

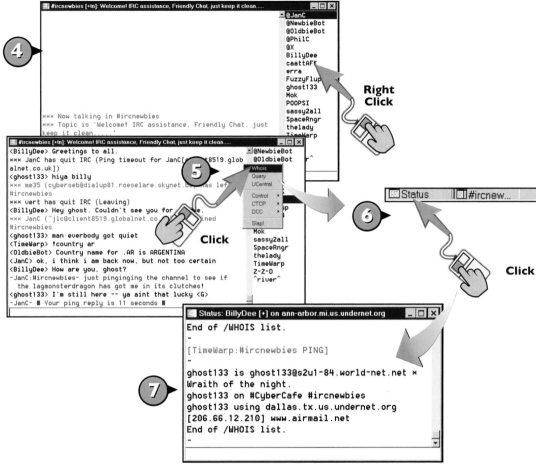

Right Click

Click

Click

④ Right-click the person's name in the list of chatters.

⑤ Choose **Whois**. (For additional information about the options on this context menu, check the Help system.)

⑥ Click the **Status** button in the mIRC status bar.

⑦ Information about the user is displayed.

✓ **Status Bar**
The status bar at the bottom of the mIRC window displays a button for each chat room you are in. The Status button returns you to the chat server screen.

End Task

Task 6: Chatting Privately

Sending Private Messages

To send a message to someone in a chat room without having the message pop up on everyone's screen, you can send a private message or create a new, private channel.

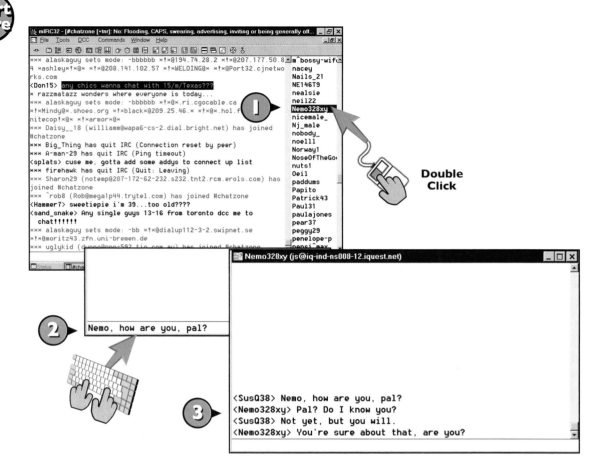

Double Click

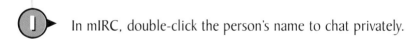

Nemo, how are you, pal?

<SusQ38> Nemo, how are you, pal?
<Nemo328xy> Pal? Do I know you?
<SusQ38> Not yet, but you will.
<Nemo328xy> You're sure about that, are you?

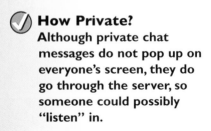

(✓) **How Private?**
Although private chat messages do not pop up on everyone's screen, they do go through the server, so someone could possibly "listen" in.

1 In mIRC, double-click the person's name to chat privately.

2 A separate chat window opens. Type your message and press **Enter**.

3 When the other person replies, the person's message pops up in the window.

Next Step

Connecting Directly

For increased privacy, you can hook up with another chatter directly through _DCC_. Short for _Direct Client-to-Client_, DCC allows two chat programs to bypass the IRC server and connect directly. You can then chat, and even exchange files, privately.

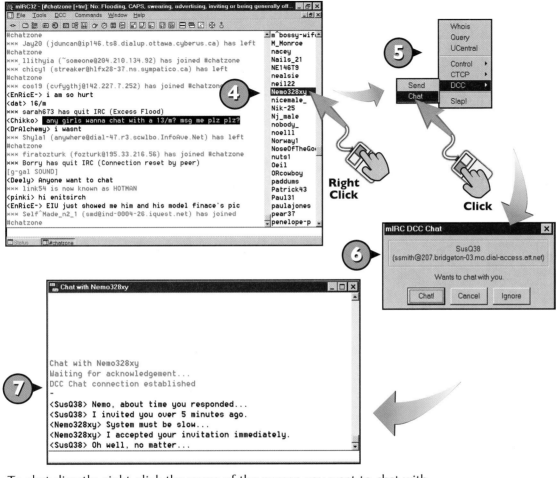

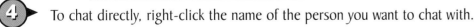

To chat directly, right-click the name of the person you want to chat with.

Point to **DCC**, and choose **Chat**.

A dialog box appears on the other person's screen, inviting the person to join you.

If the person accepts your invitation, a separate chat window appears with just the two of you.

Task 7: Exchanging Messages with AOL Instant Messenger

Installing AOL Instant Messenger

If you have friends or relatives who hang out on the Internet, you can use America Online's Instant Messenger to chat privately with them. (You do not have to join America Online.) You make a list of your friends and relatives, and Instant Messenger lets you know if they're online.

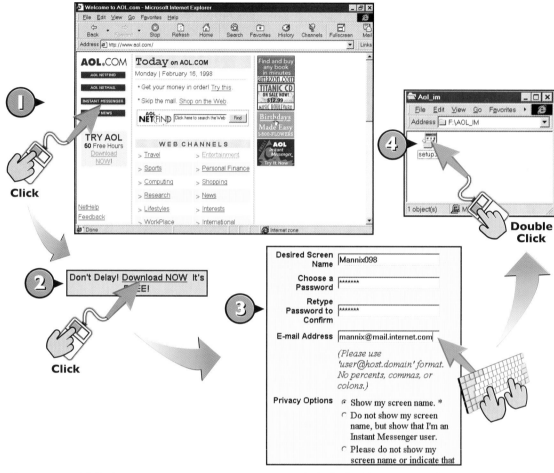

✔ **Drawback**
You have to convince all your friends and relatives to register and install Instant Messenger.

① Connect to AOL's home page at **www.aol.com**, and click the **Instant Messenger** link.

② Scroll down the page, and click the **Download Now** link.

③ Complete the registration form and follow the instructions to download the program.

④ Change to the folder in which you downloaded the Setup file, double-click the file, and follow the onscreen instructions.

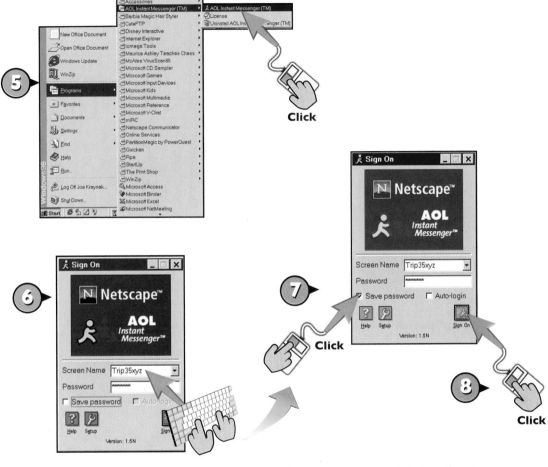

Click

Running Instant Messenger

If you want people to be able to track you down, you must be connected to the Internet, and Instant Messenger must be running. Your name will then show up on the buddy list of anyone who added you to their buddy list.

Click

Click

5 Choose **Start**, **Programs**, **AOL Instant Messenger**, **AOL Instant Messenger**.

6 Enter the screen name and password you entered when you registered for Instant Messenger.

7 Click **Save Password** to have Instant Messenger remember your login information.

8 Click the **Sign On** button.

End Task

Task 8: Sending Instant Messages

Making a Buddy List

The most useful feature of Instant Messenger is that it notifies you when friends and relatives are online. It does this by using a buddy list. You enter a person's screen name in your buddy list, and when the person connects to the Internet, Instant Messenger displays the person's screen name.

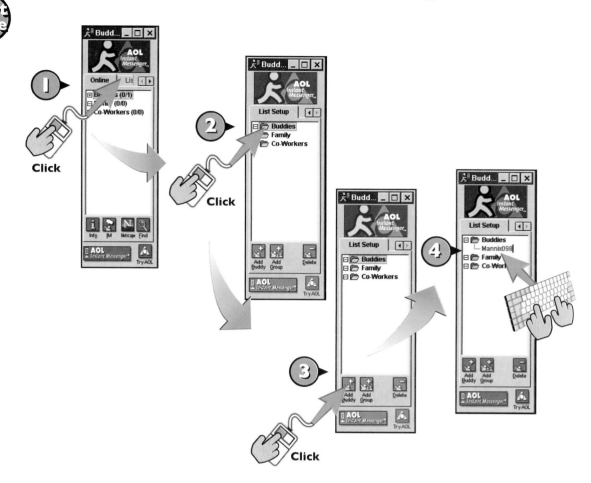

Start Here

Click

Click

Click

✓ **Find a Screen Name**
If you know the person's email address, click the **Menu** button and choose **Find a Buddy, By Email Address.**

① Click the **List** tab.

② Click the folder in which you want to insert the person's name.

③ Click the **Add Buddy** button.

④ Type the person's screen name, and press **Enter**.

Next Step

Sending an Instant Message

Whenever someone on your buddy list connects to the Internet, the person's screen name appears on Instant Messenger's Online tab. You can then choose the person's name and send a message.

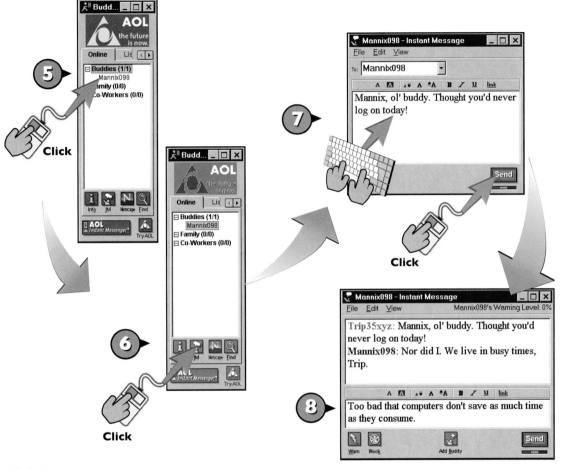

5 Click the person's screen name.

6 Click the **IM** button.

7 Type your message in the message area, and click the **Send** button.

8 The message window displays your messages along with the other person's messages.

Task 9: Exploring 3D Virtual Chat Rooms

Obtaining a 3D Chat Program

If you're tired of the same old chat, try chatting in 3D with an *avatar chat program*. With avatar chat, you take on the persona of an avatar and mingle with other avatars in three-dimensional space. To explore 3D chat rooms, you must first download and install a 3D chat program.

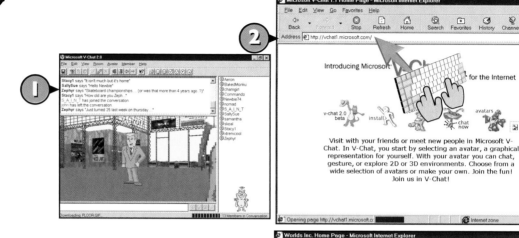

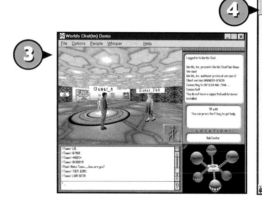

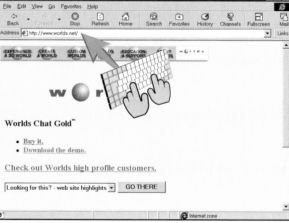

It Takes Some Power
To chat successfully in 3D, you need a fairly powerful computer and a speedy connection. Don't try this with a 14.4Kbps modem.

 Microsoft V-Chat is fun to play with, but you may not find many chatters using it.

 You can download Microsoft's V-Chat at **vchat1.microsoft.com**.

 Worlds Chat is a more popular (and powerful) 3D chat program. Think of it as the chat version of *Myst*.

 You can download a Worlds Chat demo from **www.worlds.net**. For the fancy stuff, buy the full version.

Next Step

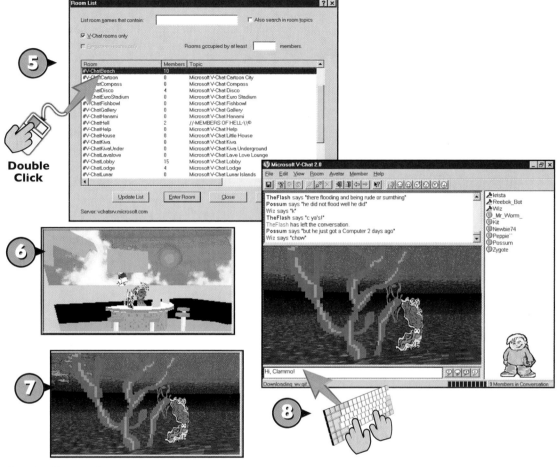

Navigating Virtual Rooms

Chatting in three dimensions is a little tough. People walk around bumping into each other. People might even walk *through* you. To take a glimpse of 3D chat and get some navigational tips, take the following tour with V-Chat.

Double Click

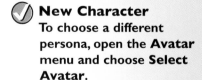

⑤ ► Run V-Chat and connect to a room.

⑥ ► Drag the mouse pointer inside the pane to move.

⑦ ► Hold down the **Ctrl** key while dragging up to fly.

⑧ ► To send a message, click inside the text box below the scene, type your message, and press **Enter**.

✓ **New Character**
To choose a different persona, open the **Avatar** menu and choose **Select Avatar.**

Internet Phone Calls and Virtual Meetings

With the proper equipment and an Internet phone program, you can call and talk to someone anywhere in the world without having to pay long-distance charges. In addition, most Internet phone programs allow you to join in virtual conferences, where participants share programs and documents, type messages, and exchange files. The tasks in this section show you just what to do to place a call over the Internet and use the conference tools.

Tasks

Task 1: Getting Started

 Start Here

Hardware Requirements

For your computer to act like a phone, it must have a sound card, speakers, and a microphone. If you plan on doing any video conferencing, you'll need a video camera. You can use a standard video camera cabled to a video capture board or a camera specially designed for video conferencing.

 Full Duplex

A full-duplex sound card can send and receive signals at the same time. A half-duplex sound card cannot send when receiving, so the conversation is much choppier.

1. Your computer must have a sound card and speakers.

2. Obtain a high-quality microphone, so your voice will sound loud and clear.

3. You can add a video camera, so the person you are talking to will be able to see you.

 Next Step

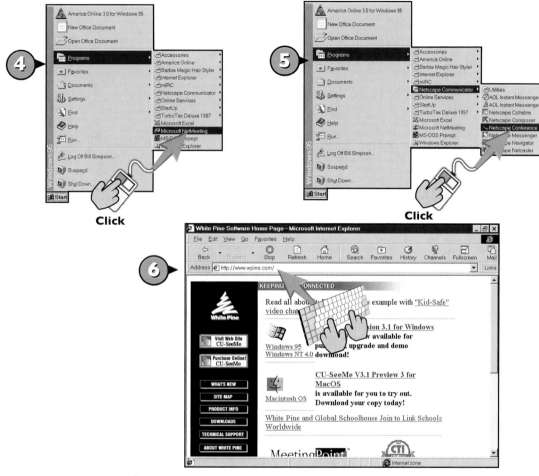

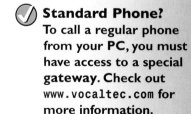

Click

Click

Required Software

Assuming you have Internet Explorer or Netscape Communicator, you have an Internet phone program: NetMeeting (Internet Explorer) or Conference (Netscape Communicator). If you plan on doing much video conferencing, consider purchasing a dedicated Internet phone program, such as CU-SeeMe.

4 ▶ To run NetMeeting, choose **Start**, **Programs**, **Microsoft NetMeeting**.

5 ▶ To run Conference, choose **Start**, **Programs**, **Netscape Communicator**, **Netscape Conference**.

6 ▶ You can purchase a copy of CU-SeeMe on the Web at **www.wpine.com**.

✓ **Standard Phone?**
To call a regular phone from your PC, you must have access to a special gateway. Check out www.vocaltec.com for more information.

Entering Connection Settings

The first time you run your Internet phone program, a series of dialog boxes appears, leading you through the setup process. You must enter your name and email address, choose the server you want to use, and adjust your microphone and speakers. (Use the same server that the person you want to call is using, or make sure you both use the default server.)

✓ Rerun Setup

To run the Setup Wizard again in Conference, choose **Help, Setup Wizard**. To change settings in NetMeeting, choose **Call, Change My Information**.

⊘ Personal Info

Omit your real phone number and address. You can insert notes instead, such as "Call me" or "Testing."

Task 2: Setting Up Your Internet Phone Program

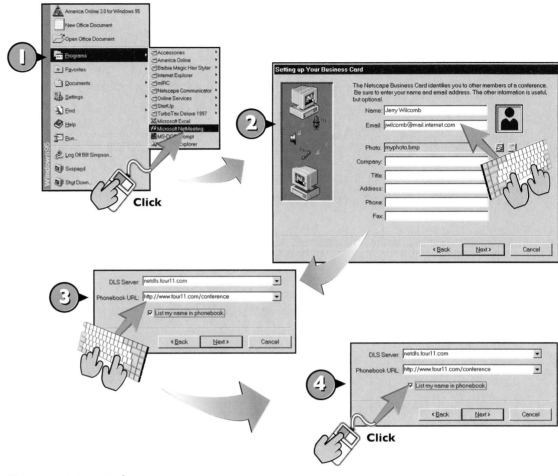

Click

Click

1 Run your Internet phone program.

2 Enter the requested information, including your name and email address (so people can call you), and click **Next**.

3 Choose the Internet phone server you want to use.

4 If you want, choose to have your name listed in a directory, so people can call you by choosing your name, and click **Next**.

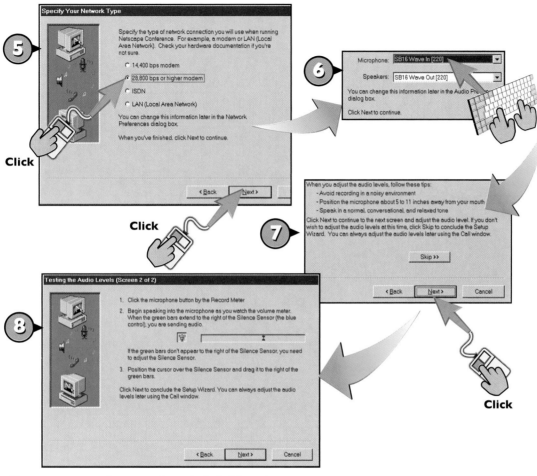

Tuning Your Hardware

The setup procedure also prompts you to specify your modem speed and to test and adjust your microphone and speakers.

5 ▶ Choose your modem speed, and click **Next**.

6 ▶ Choose the sound card to which your microphone and speakers are connected, and click **Next**.

7 ▶ When prompted to test your microphone, make sure it is turned on, and click **Next**.

8 ▶ Follow the instructions to test and adjust your microphone, and then complete the setup procedure.

 Microphone Woes
If your microphone is not working, check the Windows volume controls and make sure **Mute** is unchecked under **Microphone**.

End Task

Task 3: Calling Someone Using an Internet Phone Directory

Picking a Person to Call

When people connect to an Internet phone server, their names are added to an online directory (if they choose to have it listed). You can call a person by choosing the person's name from the directory listing.

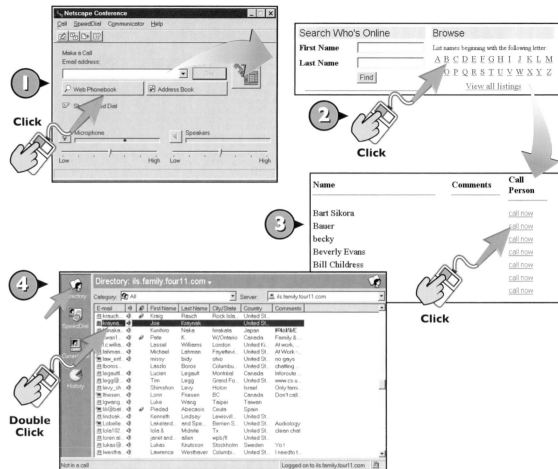

Start Here

Click

Click

Double Click

Click

✓ **Moving Directory?**
If you click the Web Phonebook button in Conference and receive a page indicating that the directory has been moved, click the link for the new location.

1 In Conference, click the **Web Phonebook** button.

2 Navigator runs and opens the FourII directory. Click a letter in the index, or click **View All Listings**.

3 Click the link for the person you want to call.

4 In NetMeeting, click the **Directory** button. Double-click a person's name to call the person.

Next Step

Conversing

When you choose to call someone, the person has the option of answering or refusing the call. If the person answers, you can immediately start talking.

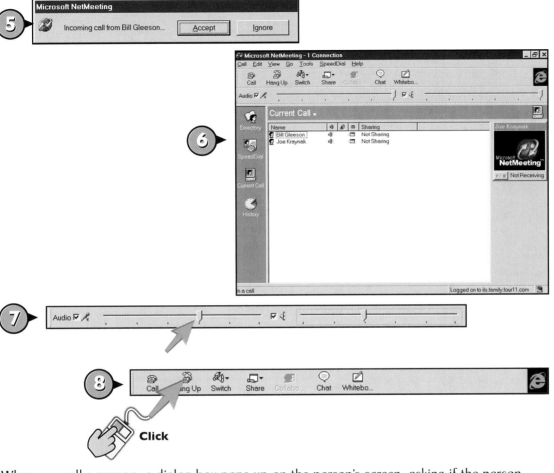

Click

(5) When you call a person, a dialog box pops up on the person's screen, asking if the person wants to take the call.

(6) Assuming the person answers, you can start talking.

(7) Use the microphone and volume controls to adjust the volume, if needed.

(8) To end the call, click the **Hang Up** button.

✓ **Testing**
Many people, like you, want to test their Internet phone program. If you don't have someone to call, check the list for people who want someone to call them.

End Task

PART

Task 4: Calling Someone Using an Email Address

Dialing an Email Address in NetMeeting

If you know the email address of the person you want to call, you may be able to dial direct, instead of searching through the online directory.

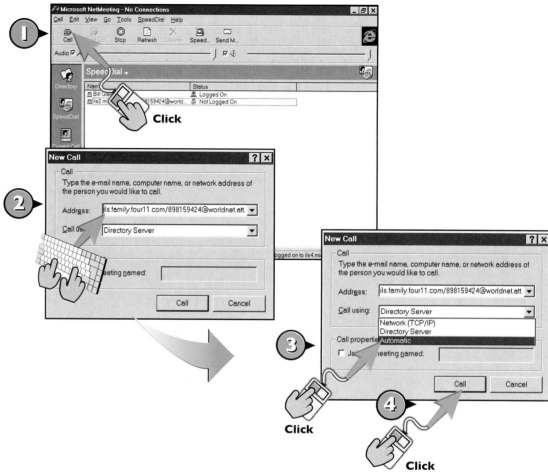

Same Server

Dialing direct works best if you are both connected to the same server. Otherwise, you must type the server's address before the email address (for example, ils.microsoft.com/bsimpson@internet.com).

① In NetMeeting, click the **Call** button.

② Type the person's email address in the text box.

③ Make sure **Automatic** is selected in the **Call Using** drop-down list.

④ Click the **Call** button.

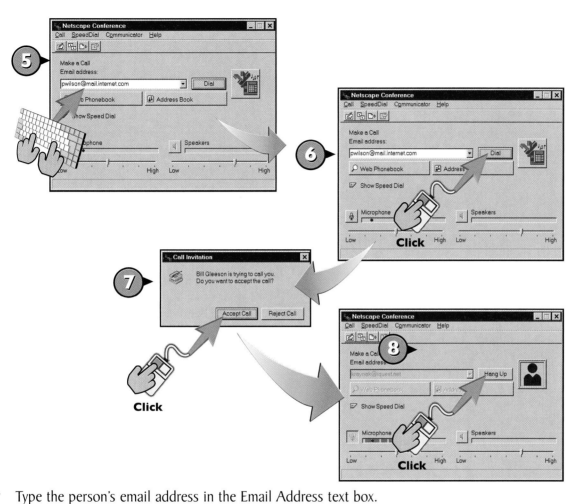

Dialing an Email Address in Conference

Although the Four11 Web page directory makes it easy to locate and call someone, Conference also lets you connect by "dialing" the person's email address.

5 Type the person's email address in the Email Address text box.

6 Click the **Dial** button.

7 After the person answers, you can start talking.

8 When you're done, click the **Hang Up** button.

Unavailable?
If the person you are calling is unavailable, a dialog box pops up allowing you to send a voice mail or text message.

End Task

Task 5: Sharing Documents with the Whiteboard

Sending a Screen Shot

NetMeeting and Conference both include a whiteboard feature that allows you to send a picture of your screen to the people you're talking to. Each person can then type and draw on the screen to communicate with the other conference participants.

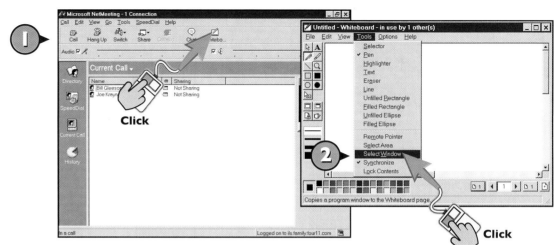

Click

Click

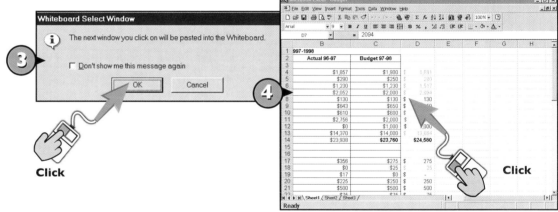

Click

Click

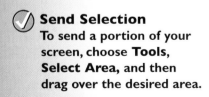

Send Selection

To send a portion of your screen, choose Tools, Select Area, and then drag over the desired area.

① ▶ Click the **Whiteboard** button and then display the document you want to send.

② ▶ Switch back to the Whiteboard and choose **Tools, Select Window**.

③ ▶ Read the Whiteboard Select Window dialog box and then click **OK**.

④ ▶ Click anywhere inside the document window.

Next Step

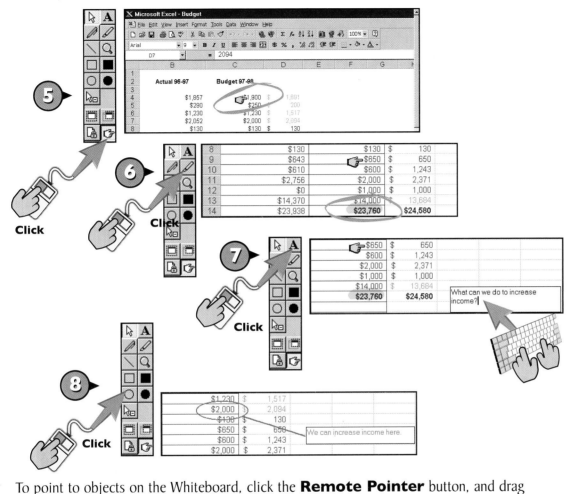

Writing on the Whiteboard

After you or another user opens a document on the Whiteboard, you can type notes, highlight key areas of the document, or even draw arrows and other shapes.

5 ▸ To point to objects on the Whiteboard, click the **Remote Pointer** button, and drag the hand icon to move the pointer.

6 ▸ To highlight objects, click the **Highlighter** button, choose the desired line thickness, and drag over the object.

7 ▸ Use the **Text** button to type notes on the Whiteboard.

8 ▸ Click any of the drawing tools, and drag on the Whiteboard to draw shapes.

Share Programs?
NetMeeting allows you to share programs as well, with the **Share Application** button. However, you should be careful not to give a stranger control of one of your programs.

 End Task

Task 6: Exchanging Text Messages with the Chat Tool

Chatting with Text

If you couldn't make a voice call (no sound card or microphone), or if your half-duplex sound card isn't up to the task, you can use the Chat tool to type messages back and forth across the Internet.

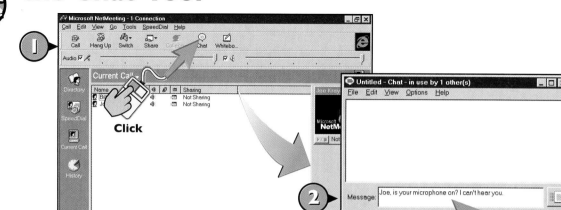

Click

 Click the **Chat** button, or choose **Tools**, **Chat**.

 Type your message, and press **Enter**.

 The message appears on your screen and on the screens of the other conference participants.

 When someone else sends a message, it appears in your chat window.

End Task

Task 7: Exchanging Files

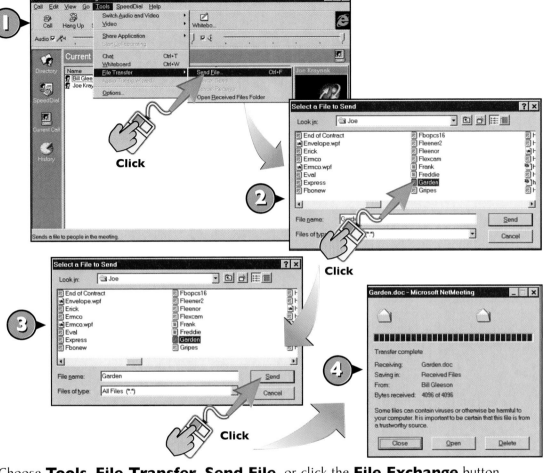

Click

Sending a File

Internet phone programs also allow you to exchange files. You send a file, and the other people in the conference can choose to accept or reject the file. This is very useful for providing up-to-date documents for people who do not have the latest versions.

Click

1 ▸ Choose **Tools**, **File Transfer**, **Send File**, or click the **File Exchange** button (in Conference).

2 ▸ Choose the file you want to send.

3 ▸ Click the **Send** button.

4 ▸ A message pops up on the recipient's screen, giving the person the option of opening the file or canceling the operation.

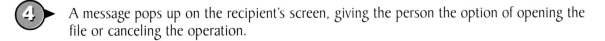

🕛 **Careful!**
Don't accept files from anyone you don't know, and don't open or run any files until you have first scanned them for viruses.

8

Creating and Publishing a Web Page

As you open Web pages, they may inspire you to create your own page and place it on the Web. Maybe you want to share your knowledge of a particular topic, advertise your business, publish your poetry, or just meet other people like you. But how do you make a Web page? And after you create it, how do you place it on the Web? These tasks show you just what to do.

Tasks

Task 1: Running a Web Page (HTML) Editor

Start Here

Understanding HTML

Behind every pretty Web page is an HTML document, a text-only document with special codes (called *tags*). (HTML is short for Hypertext Markup Language.) HTML tags control the appearance of text, insert graphics and links, and control the page layout.

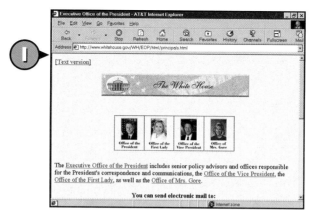

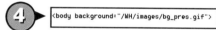

Save in One Folder
When creating a Web page, save your Web page and any associated graphics or Web pages in a single folder to make publishing the page easier.

1 ▶ A Web page looks attractive when displayed in a Web browser.

2 ▶ The Web page actually consists of a text-only document with HTML tags.

3 ▶ Paired codes tell the browser to turn enhancements, such as bold or italic, on and off.

4 ▶ Unpaired codes insert line breaks, graphics, and other objects.

Next Step

Running Your Web Page Editor

Although you can create a Web page by typing **HTML** codes in a text editor, such as Notepad, a Web page editor (called an **HTML** editor) can handle the codes for you. You format the document just as if you were using a word processor. You can use Internet Explorer's FrontPage Express or Netscape's Composer.

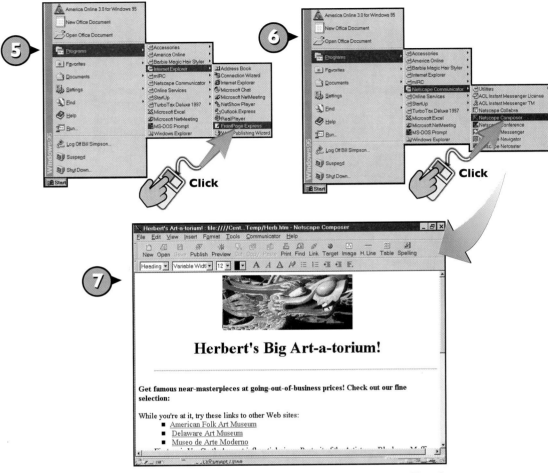

Click

Click

5 To run FrontPage Express, choose **Start**, **Programs**, **Internet Explorer**, **FrontPage Express**.

6 To run Composer, choose **Start**, **Programs**, **Netscape Communicator**, **Netscape Composer**.

7 The HTML editor looks similar to a word processor or desktop publishing program.

✓ **Other Web Page Editors**
For a more powerful Web page editor, try HotDog at www.sausage.com, or purchase Microsoft's FrontPage, a step up from FrontPage Express.

End Task

Task 2: Making a Simple Page Using a Template

Starting with a Template

The easiest way to create a Web page is to start with an existing page. If you find a Web page you like, open it in Composer or FrontPage Express and modify it to make it your own. If you have Composer, you can use existing pages, called templates, from Netscape's Web site as shown here.

(!) Get Permission
Before copying a unique Web page design, send an email message asking for permission.

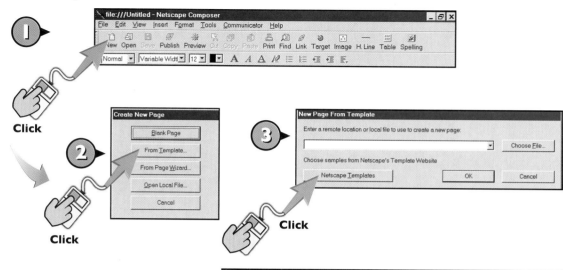

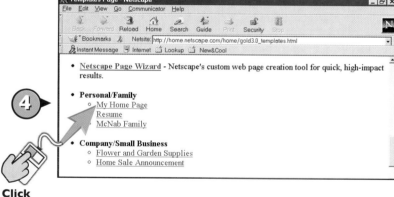

① Click the **New** button in Composer's toolbar.

② Click the **From Template** button.

③ Click the **Netscape Templates** button.

④ Scroll down the page, and click the link for the template you want to use.

Next Step

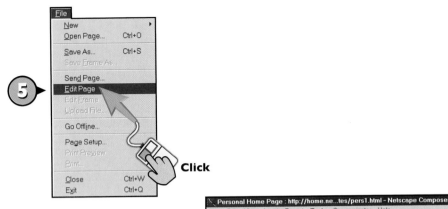

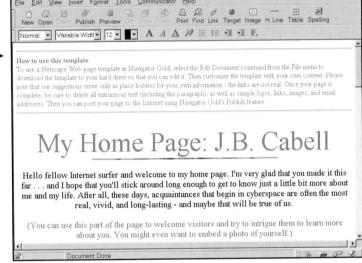

Netscape's templates are existing Web pages that Netscape has made available for anyone to modify and use. You can use these templates in Composer or whichever Web page editor you are using.

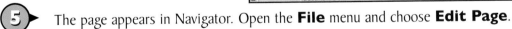

5 The page appears in Navigator. Open the **File** menu and choose **Edit Page**.

6 The page appears in Composer, where you can start editing it.

 FrontPage Express
To modify an existing Web page in FrontPage Express, open the page in Internet Explorer, and choose **Edit, Page**.

Using a Web Page Wizard

FrontPage Express and Composer both feature a Web Page Wizard that can lead you step by step through the process of creating a Web page. You simply run the Wizard and enter your preferences in a series of dialog boxes. Here, you see how to start the FrontPage Express Web Page Wizard.

Task 3: Making a Web Page with a Web Page Wizard

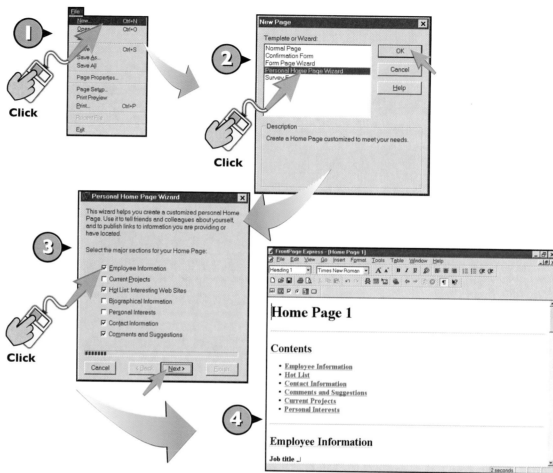

Click

Click

Click

✓ **Composer's Wizard**
To run Composer's Web Page Wizard, click the **New** button and click **From Page Wizard**. Follow the instructions at Netscape's Web site.

① Open the **File** menu and choose **New**.

② Choose **Personal Home Page Wizard** and click **OK**.

③ In each dialog box, enter your preferences and click **Next**.

④ The Wizard creates the page according to your specifications and displays it.

Task 4: Creating a Web Page with Drag-and-Drop

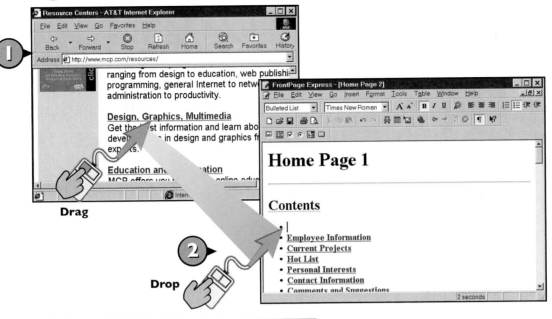

Drag

Drop

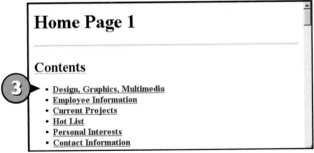

Inserting Objects with Drag-and-Drop

Most Web page editors support drag-and-drop. You can drag text, graphics, links, and other objects from your documents or from existing Web pages (displayed in your browser) and drop them on your page (displayed in your Web page editor).

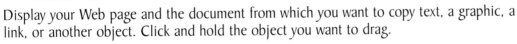

① Display your Web page and the document from which you want to copy text, a graphic, a link, or another object. Click and hold the object you want to drag.

② Drag the object onto your Web page where you want to insert the object, and release the mouse button.

③ The object appears in your page.

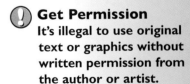

Get Permission
It's illegal to use original text or graphics without written permission from the author or artist.

Task 5: Adding and Formatting Text

Inserting and Deleting Text

Although the template or wizard provided you with a page that includes text, you will probably want to insert additional text and delete some of the existing text. Use the same techniques you use in your word processor or desktop publishing program.

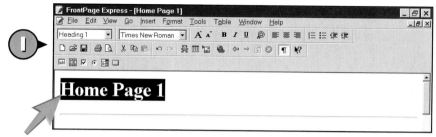

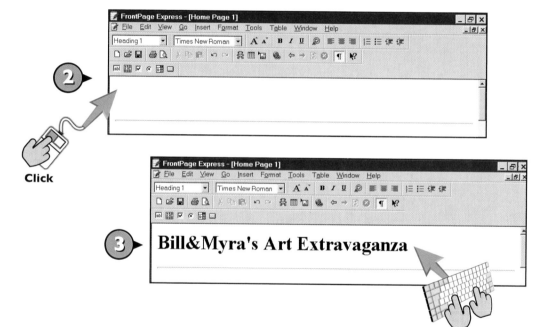

Click

✓ Cut and Paste

To cut text, highlight it and press Ctrl+X. To paste text, click where you want the text inserted and press Ctrl+V.

1 To delete text, highlight the text by dragging over it with your mouse, and then press the Delete key.

2 To insert text, click where you want the text inserted.

3 Type additional text as desired.

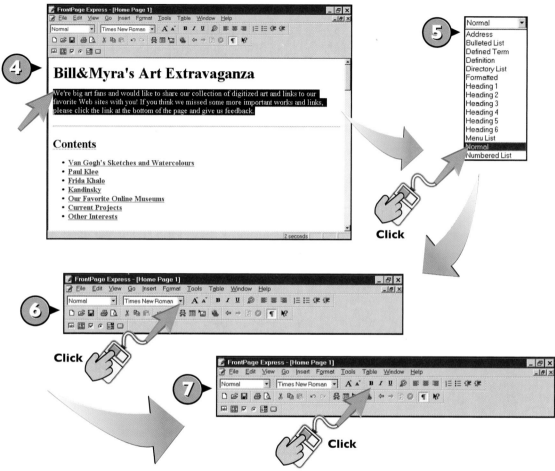

Formatting Your Text

As with any publication, you can control the appearance of text on Web pages. You can use a larger font size for headings and subheadings; make text bold, italic, or underline; and even change the color of the text. Most options are available on the Formatting toolbar.

4 Highlight the text you want to format.

5 Choose the desired paragraph style, typically one of the Heading styles or Normal (for running text).

6 Select a font style, size, or color, if you want.

7 Apply an enhancement, such as bold or italic, if desired.

Standard Formatting
Try to stick with standard fonts and formatting, so your page will look the same in most Web browsers.

Task 6: Inserting Lists

Making a Bulleted or Numbered List

Although paragraphs are useful for page introductions, people rarely spend time reading several paragraphs on a page. They open the page and quickly scan it to see if it has the information they want. To make your information easy to find (and skip), use lists.

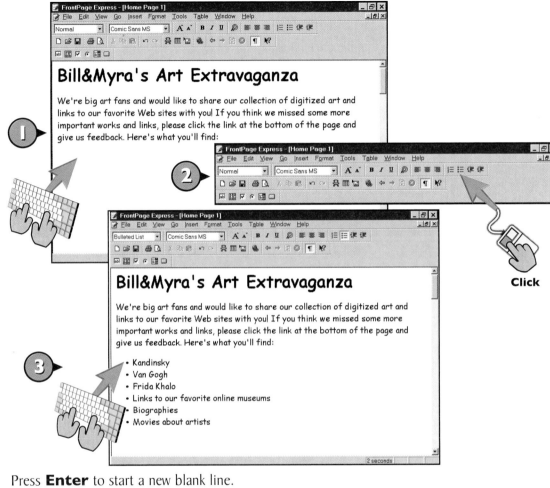

Click

Start Here

(✓) **Paragraphs->Lists**

To quickly transform short paragraphs into a list, highlight the paragraphs and click the **Bullet** or **Numbered List** button.

1 Press **Enter** to start a new blank line.

2 Click the **Bullet** or **Numbered List** button.

3 Type your list. Each time you press **Enter**, your Web editor creates a new bulleted or numbered item. Click the **Bullet** or **Numbered List** button again to turn off the feature.

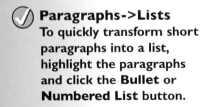

Next Step

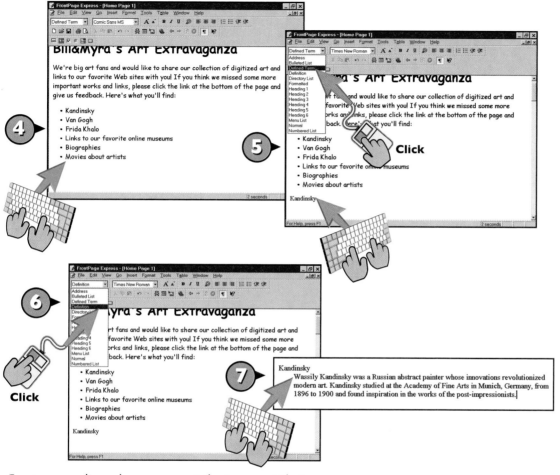

Creating Definition Lists

Although bulleted and numbered lists are most common, you should use definition lists to define terms or describe concepts. Each item in a definition list consists of a title or term followed by an indented definition or description.

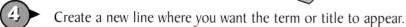

4 Create a new line where you want the term or title to appear.

5 Open the **Paragraph Style** drop-down list, choose **Desc. Title** or **Defined Term**, and type the term or title.

6 Press **Enter**, and then open the **Paragraph Style** drop-down list and choose **Desc. Text** or **Definition**.

7 Type your definition or description.

Task 7: Inserting Graphics

Start Here

Inserting Pictures

No Web page is complete without graphic illustrations. If you have a graphics program that can save files in the .GIF or .JPG format, you can create your own illustrations. Or, with permission, you can insert images from the Web into your page.

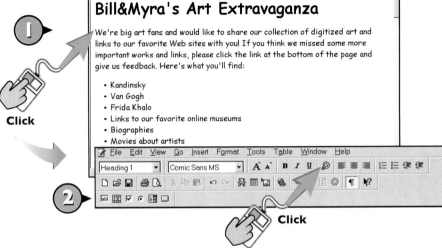

Click

Click

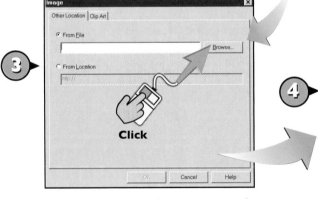

Click

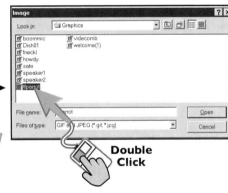

Double Click

 Pictures at Lycos
Connect to Lycos at www.lycos.com and type a word describing the type of image you need. Open the **Search for** drop-down list, and choose **Pictures**. Click **Go Get It**.

 Move the insertion point where you want the image inserted.

 Click the **Image** or **Insert Image** button.

 Click the **Browse** or **Choose File** button.

4 Change to the folder that contains the graphic file, and double-click the file's name.

 Next Step

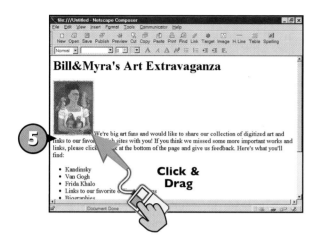

Click &
Drag

Click &
Drag

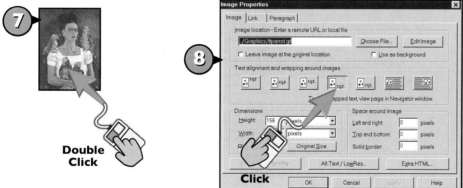

Click

Double
Click

Formatting Pictures

After inserting a picture, you can move it, resize it, or control the way text wraps around it. These steps show how to control an image in Composer. The steps are identical in FrontPage Express, but the Image Properties dialog box differs greatly from the dialog box shown in step 4. After double-clicking the image, click the **Appearance** tab.

(5)> To move the image, drag it.

(6)> To resize the image, click it and drag one of the corner handles.

(7)> To change other image properties, double-click the image.

(8)> Use the resulting dialog box to specify how text should wrap around the image.

Right-Click the Image
For additional options, right-click the image to display a context menu.

End
Task

Task 8: Creating Your Own Links

Linking to Other Pages

Without links that point to other Web pages, your Web page is a dead end, and most people won't choose to revisit. You can easily transform existing text or images into links that point to Web pages at your site or at other sites on the Web.

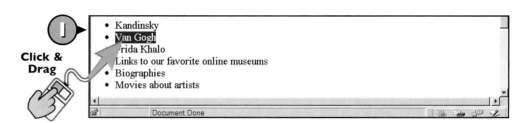

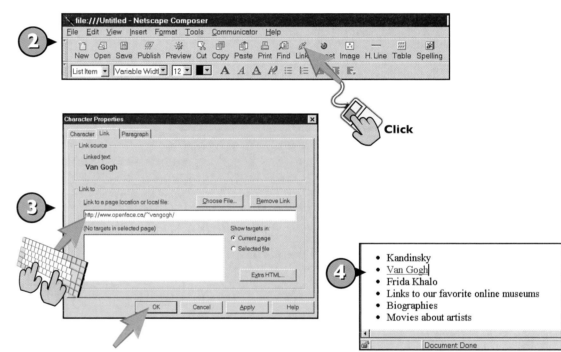

 **Add an Email Address Link**

In the address text box, type `mailto:` followed by your email address. People can then click the link to send you a message.

 Highlight the text or click the image that you want to use as your link.

 Click the **Link** button (the **Create or Edit Hyperlink** button in FrontPage Express).

 Type **http://** followed by the page address you want the link to point to, and click **OK**.

 If you used text as the link, it appears blue and underlined.

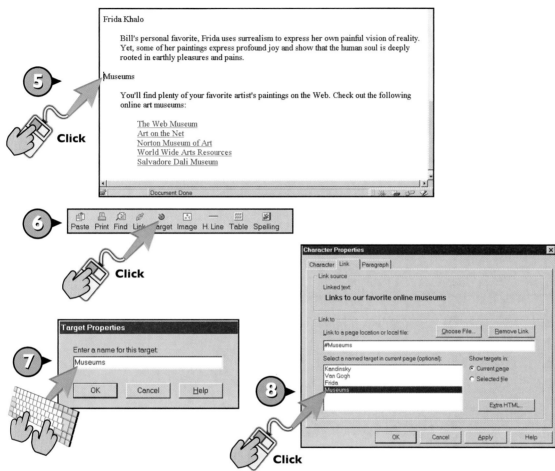

Frida Khalo

Bill's personal favorite, Frida uses surrealism to express her own painful vision of reality. Yet, some of her paintings express profound joy and show that the human soul is deeply rooted in earthly pleasures and pains.

Museums

You'll find plenty of your favorite artist's paintings on the Web. Check out the following online art museums:

The Web Museum
Art on the Net
Norton Museum of Art
World Wide Arts Resources
Salvadore Dali Museum

Document Done

5 Click

Paste Print Find Link Target Image H. Line Table Spelling

6 Click

Target Properties

Enter a name for this target:

Museums

OK   Cancel   Help

7

Character Properties

Character | Link | Paragraph

Link source

Linked text:

Links to our favorite online museums

Link to

Link to a page location or local file: Choose File...   Remove Link

#Museums

Select a named target in current page (optional):   Show targets in:

Kandinsky   ⦿ Current page
Van Gogh   ○ Selected file
Frida
Museums

Extra HTML...

OK   Cancel   Apply   Help

8 Click

Linking on the Same Page

If you have a long Web page, insert an outline of the page at the top and then transform the items in the outline into links that point to different areas on your page. You do this by inserting *bookmarks* or *targets* at the destination points and then inserting links that point to the bookmarks or targets.

5 Click to move the insertion point where you want to insert the target.

6 Click the **Target** button (Composer) or choose **Edit**, **Bookmark** (FrontPage).

7 Type a name for the target or bookmark, and click **OK**.

8 Create a link, but choose the name of the target or bookmark instead of entering a page address.

End Task

PART 8

Task 9: Using Tables to Structure Text and Graphics

Inserting a Table in FrontPage Express

Controlling the overall page layout and aligning text in columns and rows can cause problems on Web pages, because no two browsers display a page the same way. For additional control over page and text layout, consider using *tables*.

Start Here

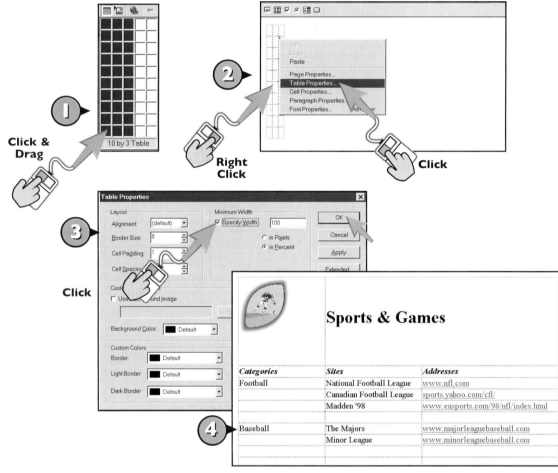

Click & Drag

Right Click

Click

Click

10 by 3 Table

Sports & Games

Categories	Sites	Addresses
Football	National Football League	www.nfl.com
	Canadian Football League	sports.yahoo.com/cfl/
	Madden '98	www.easports.com/98/nfl/index.html
Baseball	The Majors	www.majorleaguebaseball.com
	Minor League	www.minorleaguebaseball.com

✓ **Shifting Columns**

In FrontPage, the columns expand as you type. Drag over the tops of the columns, right-click the selection, choose **Cell Properties**, and set the minimum cell width to a percentage of the table width (for example, for 2 columns, use 50%).

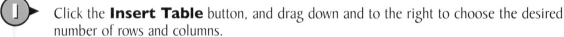

1. ► Click the **Insert Table** button, and drag down and to the right to choose the desired number of rows and columns.

2. ► Right-click the table and choose **Table Properties**.

3. ► Make sure **Specify Width** is checked, and click **OK**.

4. ► You can insert text, graphics, and links into each cell in the table.

Next Step

Click

Click

Inserting a Table in Composer

In Netscape Composer, clicking the Table button displays a dialog box that allows you to specify the desired number of columns and rows and enter other table settings. After you enter your preferences and click OK, Composer inserts the table.

(5) Click the **Table** button.

(6) Enter the desired number of columns and rows.

(7) Make sure **Equal Column Widths** is checked, enter any other desired settings, and click **OK**.

(8) You can insert text, a link, or an image into each cell.

✅ **Reformat Table**
Right-click the table and choose Table Properties to change the table settings at any time.

End Task

Task 10: Changing the Page Background and Colors

Changing the Color Scheme

Unless you specify otherwise, the browser that opens your Web page controls the colors used for the background, text, and links. You can force the browser to use a specific color scheme instead.

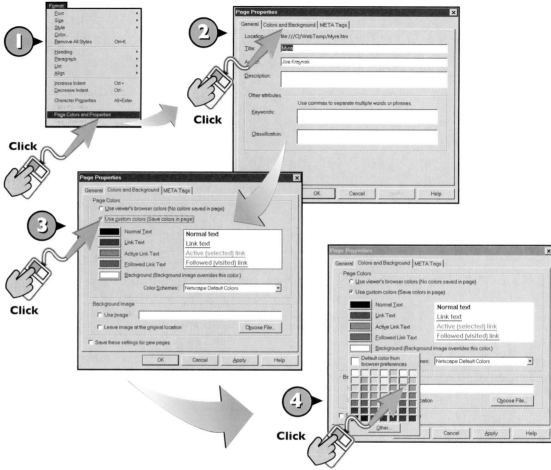

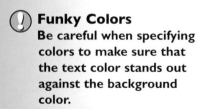

Funky Colors
Be careful when specifying colors to make sure that the text color stands out against the background color.

1 Open the **Format** menu and choose **Background** (FrontPage) or **Page Colors and Properties** (Composer).

2 Click the **Background** tab to bring it to the front, if necessary.

3 Choose the option for using custom colors, if required.

4 Click the color button for the item whose color you want to change, and click the desired color.

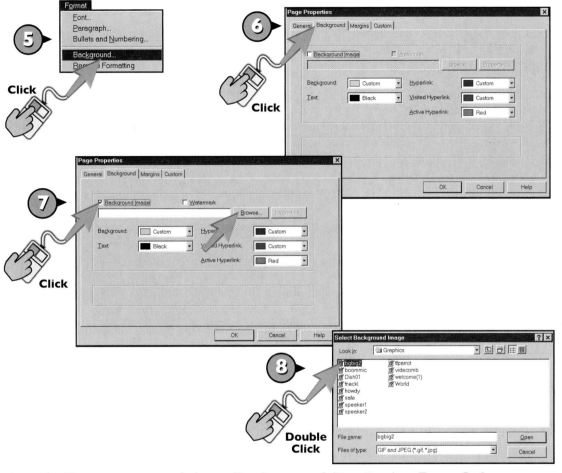

Click

Click

Click

Double Click

Using a Background Image

If you have a logo or other graphic that you want to use in place of a color background, you can insert the graphic as a background. This typically overrides any color background setting.

End Task

Page
187

---

5 Open the **Format** menu and choose **Background** (FrontPage) or **Page Colors and Properties** (Composer).

6 Click the **Background** tab to bring it to the front, if necessary.

7 Click **Background Image** or **Use Image** check box and click the **Browse** or **Choose File** button.

8 Change to the folder in which the graphic file is stored, and double-click the file's name.

Task 11: Checking Your Page

Previewing Your Page from Composer

Although your page may look fine in Composer, it may not look the same in a Web browser. You should preview your page in Navigator, check its appearance, and make sure each link works.

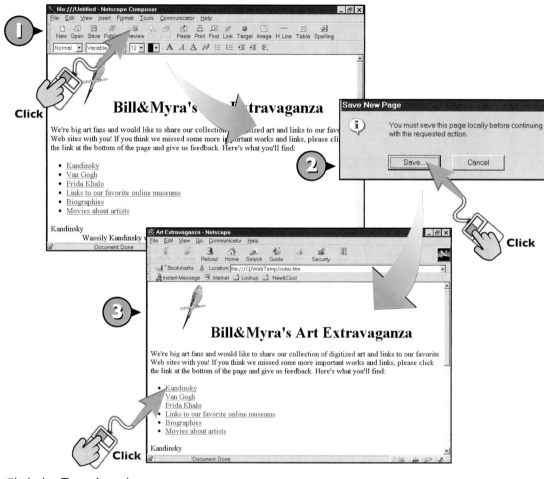

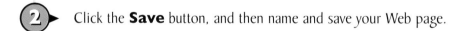

Spelling and Grammar
Read your page thoroughly before posting it on the Web, and use your Web page editor's spelling checker, if it has one (Composer does, FrontPage Express does not).

1 ▶ Click the **Preview** button.

2 ▶ Click the **Save** button, and then name and save your Web page.

3 ▶ Navigator runs and then opens and displays your Web page. Check the appearance of the page, and click each link to make sure it points to the right page.

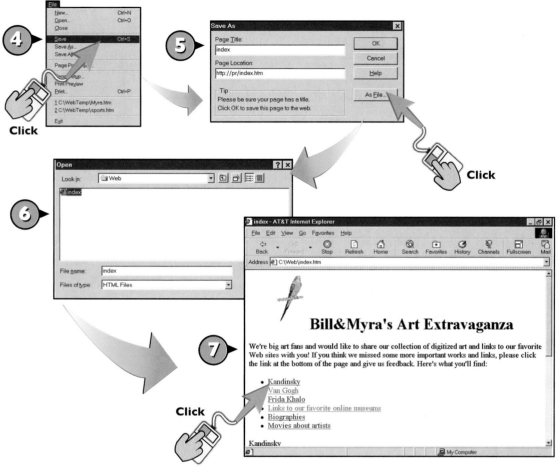

Previewing Your Page in Internet Explorer

FrontPage Express has no Preview button. You must first name and save your Web page to a folder on your hard drive. You can then open the page in Internet Explorer.

4 Open the **File** menu and choose **Save**.

5 Click the **As File** button, and save the file to one of your folders.

6 Run Internet Explorer, press **Ctrl+O**, and open the Web page file you just saved.

7 Read the page thoroughly and click each link to make sure it points to the correct Web page.

 Other Browsers
If possible, check your page with another Web browser. It may look different and reveal additional problems you need to fix.

Task 12: Finding a Place to Publish Your Page

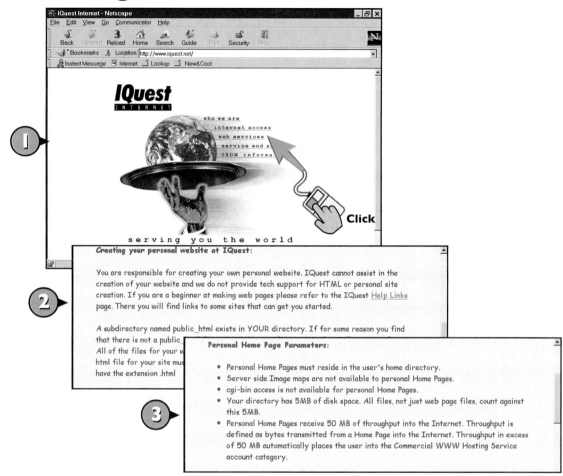

Using Your Internet Service Provider

The most obvious place to begin searching for a home for your Web page is your Internet service provider (ISP) or commercial online service (such as America Online). You may be able to obtain the information you need from your ISP's Web site, or contact your ISP by phone.

⊘ No Web Hosting?
If your ISP does not have information on the Web, call your ISP.

⊘ Commercial Online Services
Most commercial online services (including America Online) allow you to publish one Web page for free.

 Connect to your ISP's home page, and click the link for information about publishing Web pages.

 Get instructions on how to post your page, or at least obtain the address of the Web or FTP site.

 Find out the maximum amount of storage space. Most ISPs provide from 2 to 5MB, enough for a few pages and some graphics.

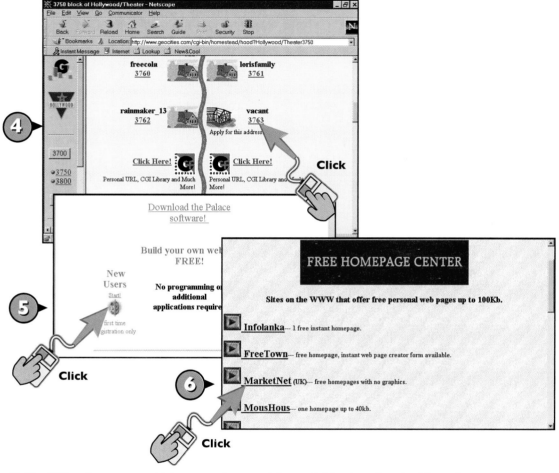

Free Sites on the Web

Many companies and organizations allow you to post a small Web page for free. The procedure for posting your page varies widely from one site to another. You may have to complete a form, email your Web page, or upload the page using FTP.

(4) At GeoCities (**www.geocities.com**), you pick a neighborhood and address for your page.

(5) At Towne Square 2000 (**townesquare.usr.com**), you can create and publish your Web page online.

(6) At the Free Home Page Center (**www.freehomepage.com**), you'll find plenty of links to additional sites.

✓ Find Free Sites
Go to www.lycos.com and search for free web page host.

❗ Read the Fine Print
Most companies that offer free Web site hosting provide the service for a limited amount of time and include additional restrictions.

Task 13: Placing Your Page on the Web

Using Microsoft's Web Publishing Wizard

FrontPage Express allows you to post your page to the Web using the **File, Save** command. However, the process is fairly complicated. It's easier to use Microsoft's Web Publishing Wizard outside of FrontPage Express.

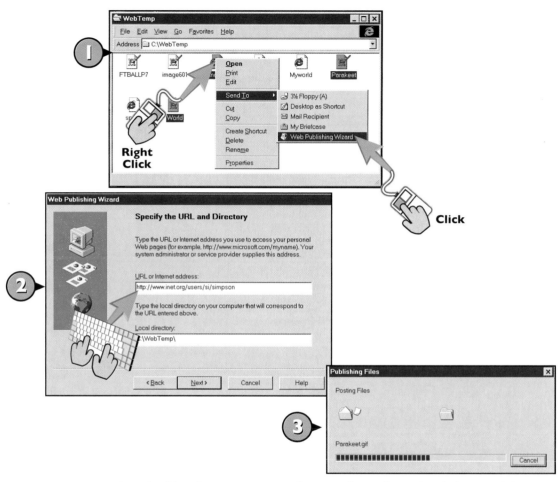

Get the Wizard
If Web Publishing Wizard is not on the menu, run Internet Explorer, open the **Help** menu, and choose **Product Updates**.

 In My Computer, select the files that you want to place on the Web. Right-click one of the selected files, and choose **Send To**, **Web Publishing Wizard**.

 Follow the onscreen instructions, entering the FTP or HTTP address your service provider told you to use.

 The wizard posts the files to the specified FTP or Web server.

Next Step

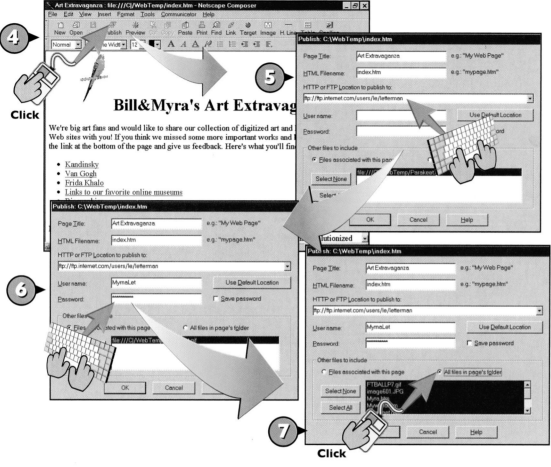

Publishing with Netscape Composer

Netscape Composer offers a simple tool for publishing your Web page and any associated graphics or other files. You click the **Publish** button, enter the requested information, and Composer handles the details.

Click

Click

4 Open the page you want to place on the Web, and click the **Publish** button.

5 Enter the HTTP or FTP address that your service provider told you to use.

6 Enter your username and password.

7 To send all the files in your folder, click **All Files in Page's Folder**. Click **OK**.

Task 14: Uploading Your Page Using an FTP Program

Uploading HTML Files

Some ISPs require that you post your files on an FTP server. They will specify the server's address and the directory in which you should place your files. They may also assign you a different username and password for accessing the FTP server. You can then use an FTP program to post your files.

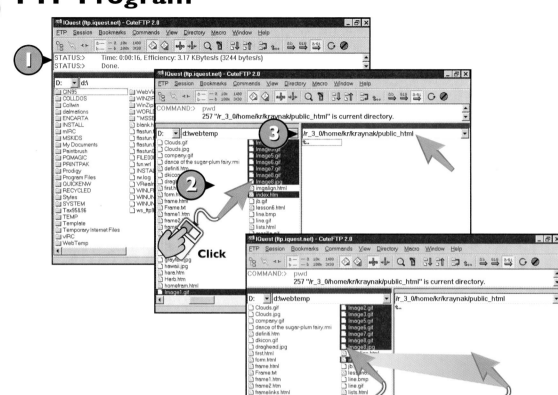

✅ Upload with Navigator

To connect to a private FTP server, go to `ftp://yourusername:yourpassword@ftp.server.address/yourdirectory`. You can then drag files from your file management program into the Navigator window to upload them.

 Run your FTP program and connect to the FTP server.

 Change to the folder in which your files are stored, and choose your Web page file and any associated files.

 Change to the specified folder on the FTP server.

 Drag the selected files into the FTP server's pane.

Task 15: Publicizing Your Page

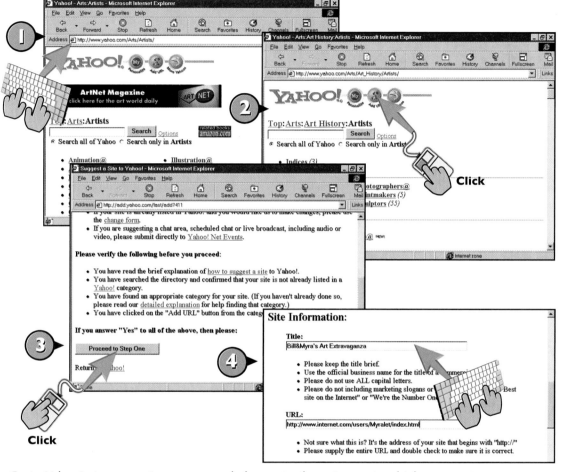

The first step in publicizing your page is to register it with various search sites, such as Yahoo!, Excite, and Lycos. Most of these sites have a link for registering your page. Here, you learn how to register with Yahoo!

Go to Yahoo! at **www.yahoo.com**, and change to the category in which you want your page listed.

Click the **Add URL** link at the top of the page.

Scroll down the page and click the **Proceed to Step One** button.

Follow the onscreen instructions, entering the requested information on the registration form.

 Submit-It
You can use Submit-It (www.submit-it.com) to announce your Web page to hundreds of sites. However, this service is not free.

Active Desktop   A Windows innovation that transforms the opening Windows screen into an information center. You can place weather maps, stock tickers, and news headlines right on the desktop and download updates automatically from the Internet.

ActiveX   A relatively new technology that allows developers to embed animated objects, games, and interactive presentations on Web pages, and enables your Web browser to play them.

address book   A list of the names and email addresses of people with whom you frequently correspond, stored in your computer's email program.

address, email   The location of a specific person's electronic mailbox on the Internet. An email address typically consists of a person's name followed by the at sign (@), followed by the domain of the service the person uses (for example, wsmith@aol.com). Email addresses are usually in all lowercase letters.

address, Web page   Also known as an URL, the location of a page on the World Wide Web.

anonymous FTP   A feature of the Internet that allows anyone to connect to and copy files from Internet sites. To connect to an anonymous FTP server, you typically sign on as guest and provide your email address as your password.

AOL Instant Messenger   A free tool offered by America Online that allows you to quickly type and send messages to your friends and relatives who also use AOL Instant Messenger.

avatar   A three-dimensional character in a virtual chat room. In some chat programs, you can take on the persona of an avatar, move your avatar from one chat room to another, mingle with other avatars, and communicate using gestures.

bookmark   1. A tool that allows you to add the names of Web pages to a menu. Instead of having to remember the address of the page to return to it, you choose it from the menu. A similar feature, called Favorites, is used in Internet Explorer (see *Favorite*). 2. An HTML tag in a Web page to which a link on the same page points (see *target*).

browser   A program that opens and displays pages on the World Wide Web.

cache   A temporary storage area in your computer's memory or hard disk that your Web browser uses to store recently opened Web pages. When you return to those pages, your Web browser can reload them more quickly from the cache than from the Web.

channel   A programmed "button" that allows you to quickly view a Web page that offers premium content. In Internet Explorer, the Channel bar allows you to flip from one Web page to another as if you were using a channel changer for a TV set.

chat   To "talk" live with another person by typing at your computer. What you type appears on the other person's screen, and what the other person types appears on your screen. You can chat on the Internet or on an online service, such as Prodigy or America Online.

chat room   A named area on the Internet or on a commercial online service where people can gather and "talk" by typing messages back and forth. Also called a *channel*.

client   A program that allows your computer to access specific Internet features. Examples of clients include Web browsers, chat programs, FTP programs, and email programs. The client connects to a *server* to access its resources.

collaborate   To work together on a project. Some Internet phone/virtual conferencing programs offer

collaboration tools, which allow two or more people in a conference to use the same program.

compact   To remove the dead space created in your email and newsgroup folders when you delete messages.

compress   To make files smaller so they take up less storage space and travel over the Internet faster.

cookie   A token that a Web server sends to your Web browser, so the server can identify you when you return. Although tokens are typically used to generate demographics and enhance your Web experience, they can also be used to record your Web habits.

DCC (Direct Client-to-Client) A chat feature that allows your computer to connect to someone else's computer directly rather than having to go through a chat server. This increases the speed at which you exchange messages and ensures greater security.

Dial-Up Networking   A feature that allows you to connect to a remote network or the Internet over a modem and telephone lines. Contrast to a *dedicated* connection, which establishes the connection through high-speed network cables.

discussion   A newsgroup conversation that consists of a posted message and all posted replies.

DNS (domain name server) A computer that your service provider uses to match domain names (such as **www.mcp.com**) with their respective IP (Internet protocol) addresses (such as 198.80.95.76) to figure out where the Web pages you request are stored.

domain   The address of a computer on the Internet. For example, the domain of the White House computer is **www.whitehouse.gov**.

download   To copy a file from a computer on the Internet to your computer.

email   An Internet feature that allows people to quickly exchange typed, postage-free messages over the Internet. Email messages reach their destination in much less time than standard mail messages.

encrypt   To scramble a message to prevent people from reading its contents in transit. Only the intended recipient can read the message if she has the proper decryption key.

extract   To decompress compressed files to use them.

FAQ (frequently asked questions)   A list of questions that people frequently ask followed by answers to those questions. By posting a FAQ, technical support people can avoid answering the same questions over and over again.

Favorite   A tool used by Internet Explorer to mark Web pages that you may want to revisit. You add your favorite Web pages to the Favorites menu and can then quickly return to them by selecting them from the menu. A similar feature, called bookmarks, is used in Netscape Navigator (see *bookmark*).

file attachment   A file that is attached to an email or newsgroup message. File attachments allow you to quickly exchange files with other people over the Internet.

filter   To route incoming email or newsgroup messages to specific folders on your hard disk based on the sender's name, subject, date, or message contents.

form   A fill-in-the-blank page on the Web. Forms make the Web more interactive, allowing you to not only access data, but to enter data, as well.

frame   A section of a Web browser window. Some Web pages divide the Web browser window into two or more frames to make it easier to navigate the page. For instance, the frame on the left may display a list of topics, while the frame on the right displays the contents of the selected topic.

freeware   Programs that are offered for free. Some Internet sites allow you to copy and use these programs at no cost. Compare to *shareware*, which you can try for free but eventually have to pay for.

FTP (file transfer protocol)   A standard language used for exchanging files over Internet connections. With an FTP program or a Web browser, you can exchange files with an FTP server on the Internet.

history list   A log of the Web sites you have recently visited. Many Web browsers track your wanderings for 20 days or more. To return to a site, you simply select it from the history list.

home page   The first page that greets you when you visit a site. Think of the home page as a mall map. The map provides links that direct you to certain areas of interest.

HTML (HyperText Markup Language)   A system of codes (called *tags*) used to control the appearance and function of Web pages. HTML tags format the Web page text and insert links, graphics, and other objects on the page.

HTTP (HyperText Transfer Protocol)   The language used for transferring Web pages over Internet connections. You will notice that every Web page address starts with http:// or https:// (s is for "secure").

IM (Instant Message)   A typed message that pops up on the recipient's screen, without the recipient having to check for it as he would have to check for email.

Internet   A global network of interconnected computers that allows people to browse the Web, exchange email, read and post newsgroup messages, chat, talk by Internet phone, and much more.

Internet Explorer   Microsoft's suite of Internet Programs, including Internet Explorer (Web browser), Outlook Express (email and newsgroups), FrontPage Express (Web page editor), and NetMeeting (virtual conferencing).

Internet phone   A technology that allows you to place a voice phone call over the Internet and avoid long-distance charges. Instead of talking on a phone, you use the speakers and microphone connected to your computer's sound card.

IRC (Internet Relay Chat)   The most popular way to chat on the Web, with IRC, you connect to a special IRC server and then pick the desired chat room or channel. If other people are in the room, you can start "talking" with them by typing messages.

ISP (Internet service provider)   A business that provides your computer with an Internet connection. The business has a computer that is directly connected to the Internet. For a fee, you can connect to this computer by network, modem, or satellite to use the Internet.

Java   A programming language commonly used on the Web to enhance Web pages and make them more interactive.

Java applet   A small application that can run on many different systems: for example, on a Macintosh running MacOS or a PC running Windows. You might encounter Java applets that let you play games, such as tic-tac-toe, or calculate refinance options for your home.

JavaScript   A system of programming codes that Web page developers can type right inside their Web pages to add animations and interactivity to their pages.

link   Highlighted text, graphics, buttons, or other objects on a Web page that a user can click to go to a different Web page.

log off   To disconnect from a server. You log off the Internet by disconnecting from your Internet service provider.

log on   To connect to a server. You log on to the Internet when you dial your Internet service provider and enter your name and password.

MIME (Multipurpose Internet Mail Extensions)   A specification for transferring non-text messages over the Internet. MIME is commonly used to transfer files attached to email and newsgroup messages.

navigate   To move around on the Internet or to control one of your programs.

Netcaster   A tool included with Netscape Communicator that allows Web sites to broadcast content to your

computer at scheduled times instead of your having to request the content.

netiquette   The rules of conduct for the Internet.

Netscape Communicator   A suite of Internet programs developed by Netscape Corporation. Communicator includes Netscape Navigator (Web browser), Messenger (email), Collabra (newsgroups), Composer (Web page editor), and Conference (Internet phone and virtual conferencing).

Netscape Navigator   A popular Web browser developed by Netscape Corporation.

newbie   A person who is new to the Internet or to a particular Internet feature.

news server   A computer that your computer connects to (using a modem or a network) to access newsgroups, read posted messages, and post your own messages.

newsgroup   An electronic bulletin board where people post messages and replies. There are more than 20,000 newsgroups on the Internet covering a wide range of topics.

newsreader   A program you use to connect to a news server, access newsgroups, read posted messages, and post your own replies and messages.

NNTP (Network News Transport Protocol)   The language used to control the transfer of newsgroup messages over the Internet.

offline   Not connected. To save time and money on the Internet, you can connect to the Internet, get your mail and anything else you want, and then disconnect and read your mail and other files offline.

plug-in   An add-on program that adds capability to a Web browser. For example, if your Web browser cannot play a certain type of audio file, you can install a plug-in that enables the Web browser to play it.

POP (Post Office Protocol)   A type of mail server that controls incoming email. To retrieve mail you have received, you connect to the POP server. To send mail, you use the SMTP server (see *SMTP*).

post   To send a message or reply to a newsgroup. The message is posted where anyone visiting the newsgroup can read it.

protocol   A set of rules that governs the exchange of data over network or Internet connections. The Internet uses several protocols, including HTTP (for Web pages), FTP (for file transfers), and POP (for email).

publish To place your Web page on a Web server making it available for other people to view.

push content A technology that allows Web sites to broadcast Web pages to you instead of waiting for you to request the pages. Push content allows you to receive content during off-hours and view it at your convenience.

search engine A tool on the Web that you can use to track down specific information and pages. Popular search sites include Yahoo! (**www.yahoo.com**), Lycos (**www.lycos.com**), Infoseek (**www.infoseek.com**), and AltaVista (**www.altavista. digital.com**).

security A system for preventing unauthorized access to your system, information you transmit, and your identity, and for preventing undesired content (such as viruses) from reaching your system.

self-extracting A compressed file that decompresses when you run it.

server A typically powerful computer on the Internet or on a network that other computers connect to in order to use its resources. For example, a Web server stores pages that Web browsers can open and display.

shareware Programs that you can use for a limited time for free but must pay for if you continue using them after the trial period. You can find plenty of shareware on the Internet.

SMTP (Simplified Mail Transfer Protocol) A language used for transferring email messages from one computer to another over the Internet.

subscribe 1. To set up your Web browser to download Web pages automatically during specified times, so you don't have to wait for the pages later. 2. To add a newsgroup to a short list of newsgroups, so you can quickly find it later.

surf To move from one page to another on the Web.

table A grid consisting of rows and columns that intersect to form boxes, called *cells*. Tables are commonly used to control the overall layout of Web pages.

tag A code that formats Web page text, specifies the colors used on the page, or inserts graphics, audio clips, video clips, or other objects on the page.

target A specific area on a Web page that a link points to. Targets are typically used to help navigate long Web documents. A list of topics at the top of the page may link to targets farther down the page.

thread A list of related newsgroup or email messages. Newsreaders commonly group posted messages by thread, so you can easily follow a discussion.

upload To copy a file from your computer to another, remote, computer.

URL (Uniform Resource Locator) Pronounced "earl," an URL is an address of a page or file on the Internet.

Usenet Short for User's Network, Usenet is a group of interconnected computers responsible for managing the exchange of messages posted in newsgroups.

user profile Information that a user enters about himself or herself. In some chat rooms, you can check a user's profile to learn more about the person. However, profiles typically provide cryptic generalities or outright lies.

username The name a person uses to identify himself to another system. You typically enter your username and password to connect to the Internet or to access your email.

virus Computer code that is designed as a prank, nuisance, or instrument of destruction.

VRML (Virtual Reality Modeling Language)
A programming language that allows Web developers to create three-dimensional, interactive worlds.

Web   Short for the *World Wide Web*, the Web is a global group of inter-connected computers that store Web pages. With a Web browser, you can skip from one computer to another, and from page to page, by entering page addresses and clicking links.

whiteboard   A tool used in virtual conferencing programs that allows you to send a picture of your screen to everyone in the conference and then write notes on it.

Wizard   An online tutor that leads you step-by-step through the process of performing a complex task. Wizards typically display a series of dialog boxes prompting you to enter your preferences.

World Wide Web   See *Web*.

Symbols

A

B

C

D

pages (Web), *see* **Web pages**

P

Q-R

S